SCHOLASTIC

BIG DAY for PreK™

Implementation Guide

Copyright © 2010 by Scholastic Inc.   All rights reserved.   Published by Scholastic Inc.   Printed in the U.S.A.

ISBN-13: 978-0-545-29352-5
ISBN-10: 0-545-29352-9

SCHOLASTIC, SCHOLASTIC BIG DAY FOR PREK, BOOKFLIX,
and associated logos are trademarks and/or registered trademarks of Scholastic Inc.
CLIFFORD and associated logos are trademarks and/or registered trademarks of Norman Bridwell.
Other company names, brand names, and product names are the property and/or trademarks of their respective owners.

1 2 3 4 5 6 7 8 9 10   40   19 18 17 16 15 14 13 12 11 10

Table of Contents

Dear Big Day for PreK Educator,

Early education helps children build a strong foundation for future social and academic success. Big Day for PreK is a comprehensive and engaging curriculum that ensures that every day is a "big day" for young learners. This new and exciting program embraces children's natural curiosity; guides their physical, social-emotional, and intellectual development; and prepares them for success in school and in life.

Grounded in responsive, integrated instruction, Big Day for PreK provides a comprehensive curriculum for full- or half-day that engages children with intentional play and theme-based learning in key domains including social-emotional development, oral language, literacy, mathematics, science, social studies, art, technology, and physical development. From the extensive collection of classic and contemporary children's literature and nonfiction texts to the innovative Web-based technology that brings children, teachers, and families together—Big Day for PreK has it all!

In today's training, you will:
- Reflect on the founding principles behind Big Day for PreK.
- Experience the Big Day for PreK curriculum and explore the teaching tools and resources.
- Plan your classroom layout and create a daily schedule.
- Get hands-on with Teacher Space and BookFlix!
- Understand how to monitor developmental progress and guide children toward kindergarten readiness.
- Learn tips for preparing and managing your classroom, welcoming children and families, and starting the school year!

This Implementation Guide and the training today will provide you with all the resources and tools necessary for starting a "big" year with Big Day for PreK!

Thank you for joining us for today's training and for your commitment to our youngest learners!

Sincerely,

Ernesto Rodriguez

Ernesto Rodriguez
National Early Childhood Consultant
Scholastic Education

Full-Day Agenda

10 minutes		**Welcome and Introductions**
25 minutes		**Introducing** *Big Day for PreK*
60 minutes		**Making Learning Bigger!** • Hands-On: Experiencing Circle Time • Hands-On: Learning in Small Groups • Hands-On: Using the Teaching Guides

Break

60 minutes		**Managing Your Day** • Hands-On: Planning Your Classroom Layout • Hands-On: Scheduling Your Day • Hands-On: Managing Your Day Online
60 minutes		**Building Literacy From School to Home** • Hands-On: Reading Beyond the Book • Hands-On: Reading Online With BookFlix • Hands-On: Exploring Resources on Family Space

Lunch

40 minutes	**Exploring Teacher Space Online** • Setting Up Classes • Communicating With Families • Downloading Tools and Resources
40 minutes	**Watching Children Learn and Grow!** • Using Checklists, Records, and Portfolios • Measuring Developmental Progress • Getting Children Kindergarten Ready!

Break

30 minutes	**Starting a Big Year!** • Preparing Your Classroom • Welcoming Families and Children • Starting Theme 1
10 minutes	**Questions and Evaluation**

Half-Day Agenda

10 minutes		**Welcome and Introductions**
15 minutes		**Introducing *Big Day for PreK***
40 minutes		**Making Learning Bigger!** • Hands-On: Experiencing Story Time • Hands-On: Learning in Small Groups • Hands-On: Using the *Teaching Guides*
30 minutes		**Managing Your Day** • Hands-On: Planning Your Classroom Layout • Hands-On: Scheduling Your Day

Break

40 minutes		**Planning and Communicating Online** • Hands-On: Managing Your Day Online • Hands-On: Reading Online With BookFlix • Hands-On: Exploring Resources on Family Space
20 minutes		**Watching Children Learn and Grow!** • Using Checklists, Records, and Portfolios • Measuring Developmental Progress
15 minutes		**Starting a Big Year!** • Preparing Your Classroom • Starting Theme 1
10 minutes		**Questions and Evaluation**

Program Overview

Hooray for *Big Day for PreK!*

Big Day for PreK *prepares young learners for kindergarten and beyond through intentional and engaging learning experiences grounded in the best research and teaching practices.*

The Importance of PreK

Research indicates that high-quality prekindergarten programs play a critical role in preparing students for school and for life. Because of this, more states are paying increasing attention to improving school readiness by investing in and developing standards for quality early childhood programs (Rhode Island KIDS COUNT, 2005).

Big Day for PreK is a high-quality, comprehensive early education program that reflects the best research and practices on how children learn and grow.

Approach to Teaching and Learning

Big Day for PreK embraces children's natural curiosity and encourages them to learn, play, and engage with the world around them. Daily instructional activities in *Big Day for PreK* are organized into three ways of learning:

Big Experiences

Each day has three theme-driven, whole-group integrated learning experiences that introduce and teach the most important skills and concepts. For each Big Experience taking place during **Circle Time** or **Story Time**, the *Teaching Guides* include three additional activities to deepen understanding as well as guidance to identify children who might benefit from one-to-one support.

Small Group Instruction

Each day includes a **Small Group Instruction** activity that builds on content and provides children with direct, intentional literacy and mathematics instruction as well as a **Small Group Intervention** activity for children who would benefit from further practice.

Learning Centers

Learning Centers extend theme learning and provide children a daily opportunity for intentional play, social interaction, and independent exploration. Each *Teaching Guide* provides guidance for setting up theme-specific activities in eight Learning Centers: Blocks & Building, Creativity, Dramatic Play, Math, Reading & Listening, Science, Technology, and Writing.

5 Big Research Principles

Research shows that quality early childhood education not only helps young learners develop a strong foundation for success in school, but also for success in life. Read and reflect on the following five "big" research-based principles behind *Big Day for PreK*.

Big Principles	Reflection
1 Social-Emotional Development It is important that children develop the behaviors and skills that will enable them to function productively and collaboratively (National Research Council, 2001).	*One important life skill children learn in PreK is . . .*
2 Language Development It is important to engage children in meaningful language interactions throughout the day by modeling and reinforcing conversation, vocabulary, and sentence structure (Albert Shanker Institute, 2009; Snow et al., 1995).	*One opportunity for engaging children in meaningful conversation during the day is . . .*
3 Integrated Learning It is important to teach the *whole* child, with integrated learning experiences in key domains such as social-emotional development, mathematics, literacy, science, fine arts, and physical development (National Scientific Council on the Developing Child, 2008).	*Teaching the whole child—heart, body, and mind—is important because . . .*
4 Responsive Instruction It is important to continuously monitor children's learning and developmental progress in order to identify needs, plan interventions, and celebrate achievements (National Research Council, 2008; Sandall, McLean, & Smith, 2000).	*Two opportunities for observing children's growth and learning could be . . .*
5 Partnership With Families It is important to form a respectful partnership with families and regularly communicate their children's learning and progress (Halgunseth et al., 2009; Strickland & Riley-Ayers, 2006).	*One way I plan to build a positive home-school connection is . . .*

Meeting the Authors and Advisors

Big Day for PreK **was developed with the expertise and experience of nationally recognized researchers and practitioners.**

Senior Author

Anne Cunningham, Ph.D.
Professor, Cognition and Development
University of California, Berkeley; Berkeley, California

Dr. Cunningham is nationally recognized for her research on literacy and development in early childhood. She examines the cognitive and motivational processes underlying reading ability and the interplay of context, development, and literacy instruction. Dr. Cunningham has served on several early childhood expert panels including the National Early Literacy Panel. Her expertise informed the entire program with specific emphasis on phonological awareness, alphabet knowledge, assessment, and professional development for the *Big Day for PreK* curriculum.

Program Authors

Nicole Andrews, Ed.D.
Assistant Professor, Early Childhood Mathematics
University of Houston; Houston, Texas

Dr. Andrews's research has primarily focused on children's mathematics, specifically spatial ability in young children. Additionally, she focuses on the professional development of preservice and inservice teachers. Dr. Andrews's expertise in early childhood mathematics informed the development of the mathematics domain of the *Big Day for PreK* curriculum.

María Elena Argüelles, Ph.D.
Researcher and Educational Consultant
Miami, Florida

Dr. Argüelles specializes in the areas of early reading instruction and reading instruction for English language learners. Dr. Argüelles has worked for the Central Reading First Regional Technical Assistance Center at the University of Texas, Austin, and as a reviewer for the Florida Center for Reading Research. Her insights into instruction for English language learners contributed to the development of support for those students in the *Big Day for PreK* curriculum.

Julie Washington, Ph.D.
Professor, Language and Literacy Initiative
Georgia State University; Atlanta, Georgia

Dr. Washington's research addresses language and literacy development in diverse populations. With preschoolers, her work has focused on understanding and improving the emergent literacy skills necessary to support later reading proficiency in high-risk groups. Her insights informed the development of the oral language, vocabulary, and emergent reading domains of the *Big Day for PreK* curriculum.

Curriculum Consultants

Antonio Fermín, Ph.D.

Early Childhood
Music Consultant

New York, New York

Mary Packard

Educational Language
Consultant

Ann Arbor, Michigan

Linda M. Platas, Ph.D.

Specialist, Institute of
Human Development

University of California, Berkeley
Berkeley, California

**Ana Laura Rodríguez-
García, Ph.D.**

Assistant Professor,
Early Childhood Education

University of Texas, Brownsville
Brownsville, Texas

Program Advisors

Francie Alexander

Senior Program Advisor,
Chief Academic Officer

Scholastic Inc.
New York, New York

Ernesto Rodriguez

National Early Childhood
Consultant

Scholastic Inc.
Austin, Texas

M'Liss Brockman

Early Childhood
Educator

New Braunfels, Texas

Cynthia Chavez

Early Literacy Consultant

El Paso, Texas

Lucille Dunkin

Early Childhood Educator

New Canaan, Connecticut

Linda Koons Nuñez

Early Childhood Editorial
Consultant

Chapel Hill, North Carolina

Teacher Reviewers

Maggie Donovan
Vero Beach, FL

Teresita Gomez
El Centro, CA

Jane Helena Nieves
Los Altos, CA

Terrie Olstowski
Imperial, CA

Kati Zsilavecz
Bethlehem, PA

Theme Learning Throughout the Year

Big Day for PreK *is a comprehensive, year-long curriculum organized into eight engaging themes to develop children's knowledge and skills through hands-on experience, purposeful play, and teacher-led instruction.*

THEME	**1** Ready for School!	**2** My Family	**3** Our Community	**4** Awesome Animals
SOCIAL-EMOTIONAL FOCUS	Cooperation	Kindness	Responsibility	Attention
KNOWLEDGE FOCUS	Children learn the expectations, routines, and behaviors of school.	Children learn about family members, family roles, and unique qualities of families.	Children learn about the role of the community in their lives and the importance of good citizenship.	Children learn about life science through the exploration of animals and animal life cycles.
WEEK 1 BIG Ideas	**My School** — I am getting to know my school.	**Who's in My Family?** — I am an important part of my family.	**Places We Go** — I visit many places in my community.	**All Kinds of Animals** — I live in a world full of animals.
WEEK 2 BIG Ideas	**Making Friends** — I will make friends at school.	**We Take Care of Each Other** — I love my family and they love me.	**People We Meet** — The workers in my community help everyone.	**Animal Homes** — Animals have a home just like me.
WEEK 3 BIG Ideas	**Learning Together** — I work and play with my friends at school.	**Family Fun** — I share special times with my family.	**Things That Move** — Transportation is for doing jobs and getting around my community.	**Creepy, Crawly Insects** — I am very curious about bugs.
WEEK 4 BIG Ideas	**Getting Along** — I know how to share and I care about the feelings of others.	**All Kinds of Families** — Every family is unique.	**Going Green!** — I can make a difference.	**Animals Grow and Change** — Animals grow and change just like me.

Big Day for PreK Professional Handbook

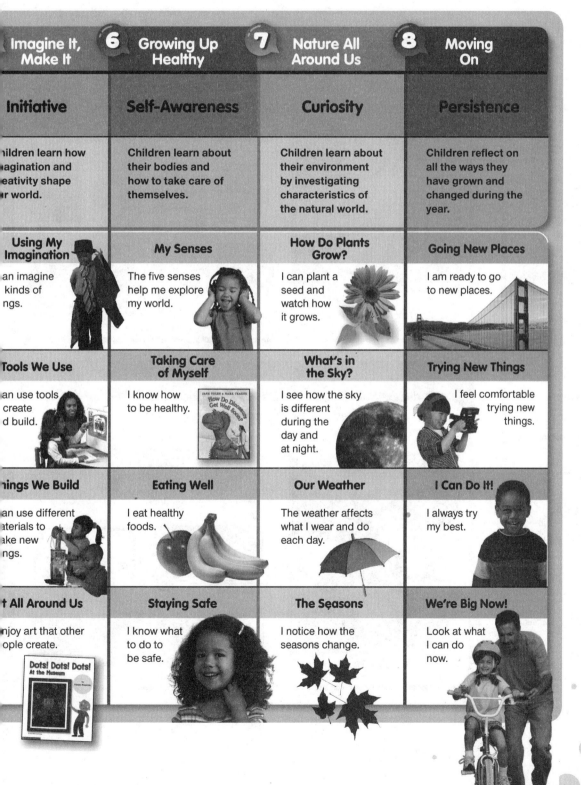

Imagine It, Make It	6 Growing Up Healthy	7 Nature All Around Us	8 Moving On
Initiative	**Self-Awareness**	**Curiosity**	**Persistence**
hildren learn how agination and eativity shape r world.	Children learn about their bodies and how to take care of themselves.	Children learn about their environment by investigating characteristics of the natural world.	Children reflect on all the ways they have grown and changed during the year.
Using My Imagination an imagine kinds of ngs.	**My Senses** The five senses help me explore my world.	**How Do Plants Grow?** I can plant a seed and watch how it grows.	**Going New Places** I am ready to go to new places.
Tools We Use an use tools create d build.	**Taking Care of Myself** I know how to be healthy.	**What's in the Sky?** I see how the sky is different during the day and at night.	**Trying New Things** I feel comfortable trying new things.
hings We Build an use different aterials to ake new ngs.	**Eating Well** I eat healthy foods.	**Our Weather** The weather affects what I wear and do each day.	**I Can Do It!** I always try my best.
t All Around Us njoy art that other ople create.	**Staying Safe** I know what to do to be safe.	**The Seasons** I notice how the seasons change.	**We're Big Now!** Look at what I can do now.

Getting to Know the Materials

Big Day for PreK *includes all the necessary resources to help you create and manage a purposeful and fun learning environment that meets the needs of all young learners.*

Teacher Welcome Kit

Essential Tools for Getting Started

Professional Handbook

Technology Portfolio*
- Teacher Space
- Family Space
- BookFlix
- Professional Development

BookStix™

Audiobooks CDs*

Be Big in the Classroom Poster*

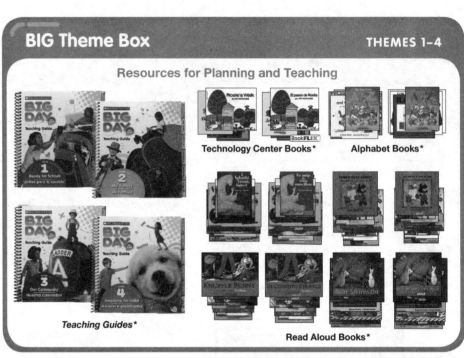

BIG Theme Box
THEMES 1–4

Resources for Planning and Teaching

Teaching Guides*

Technology Center Books*

Alphabet Books*

Read Aloud Books*

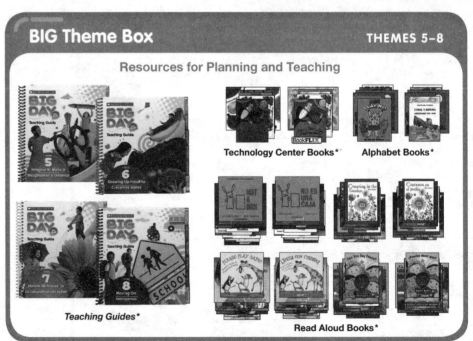

BIG Theme Box
THEMES 5–8

Resources for Planning and Teaching

Teaching Guides*

Technology Center Books*

Alphabet Books*

Read Aloud Books*

* *Big Day for PreK* is published in two editions: English and English/Spanish. Spanish components are included in the English/Spanish edition.

BIG Book Box
ENGLISH
Big Books and Lap Books for Sharing

BIG Book Box
SPANISH*
Big Books and Lap Books for Sharing

Little Book Box
ENGLISH
Little Books for Little Hands

Little Book Box
SPANISH*
Little Books for Little Hands

BIG Wall Chart Box
Wall Charts for Building Oral Language*

BIG Learning Box
Materials for Building Language and Content-Area Knowledge

Clifford® Posters*

Clifford® Books*

Clifford® Puppet

Songs and Fingerplays Book and CDs*

Manipulatives Kit
- Snap Cubes
- Attribute Blocks
- Pattern Blocks
- Balance Set and Bears
- Magnifiers
- Magnetic Healthy Food Kit
- Magnetic Numbers

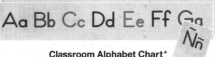

Classroom Alphabet Chart*

Math Mats*

Science Posters*

Letter Cards*

Picture Cards*

Number Cards

Magnetic Alphabet Letters*

Magnetic Alphabet Boards

Letter Vest and Vest Pocket Letters

* *Big Day for PreK* is published in two editions: English and English/Spanish. Spanish components are included in the English/Spanish edition.

Introducing *Big Day* Online

Web-based technology brings teachers, children, and families together in support of learning at school and at home.

Teacher Space

Teacher Space is your online learning management system. From any computer with an Internet connection, you can log in to Teacher Space (**http://bigday.scholastic.com**) to:

- Create and manage your class roster.
- Plan and customize lessons.
- Access teaching materials (e.g., *Teaching Guides, Professional Handbook, Songs and Fingerplays*) digitally.
- Download and print resources.
- Print assessments, enter data, and run reports to monitor children's growth and progress.
- Communicate with families online.
- View correlations to standards.
- Engage children with interactive online books with BookFlix.
- Access online professional development.

ACCESS your roster, view data at a glance, and look up parent contact information online.

CUSTOMIZE your week's activities and objectives.

DOWNLOAD assessment tools to monitor children's learning year-round.

POST messages on Family Space to maintain the home-school connection all year long.

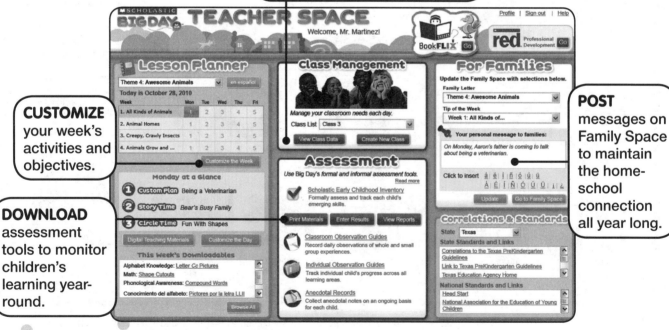

Teacher Space Home Page

Family Space

Big Day for PreK recognizes the importance of partnering with families to support children's growth and learning. Family Space is a bilingual website that helps teachers and families stay connected throughout the year. Families can log in to Family Space **(http://big dayfamily.scholastic.com)** anytime, anywhere to:

- Read personal messages from the teacher.
- Learn about theme topics and classroom activities.
- Enjoy Fun With Clifford® online activities.
- Access BookFlix, the exciting and interactive online literacy resource.
- Download books and printable resources to extend children's learning at home.
- Access all materials on the site in English and Spanish.

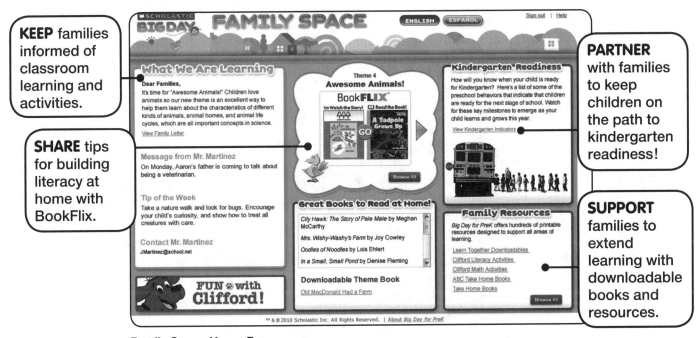

KEEP families informed of classroom learning and activities.

SHARE tips for building literacy at home with BookFlix.

PARTNER with families to keep children on the path to kindergarten readiness!

SUPPORT families to extend learning with downloadable books and resources.

Family Space Home Page

Reading Online With BookFlix

Big Day for PreK includes unlimited access to BookFlix, the online literacy resource that brings books to life for young learners! BookFlix for *Big Day for PreK* pairs classic video storybooks with nonfiction eBooks related to each of the eight program themes. Children can read fiction-nonfiction pairs such as:

- *Owen* and *We Help Out at School*
- *Is Your Mama a Llama?* and *Animal Babies*
- *Harold and the Purple Crayon* and *Where Can Art Take You?*

With one-click access from Teacher Space and Family Space, teachers, children, and families can easily use BookFlix to turn any environment into a learning environment! When logged in to BookFlix **(http://bigdaybookflix.scholastic.com)**, children can:

- See fictional stories come alive with a video storybook.
- Read nonfiction eBooks with language support.
- Enjoy fun literacy-building activities.
- Learn more about the authors.
- Explore child-friendly Web links related to the theme topics.

READ books and view activities in both English and Spanish!

ACCESS fiction-nonfiction Reading Pairs related to each theme.

BookFlix Home Page

Exploring a Theme

Launching a Theme

Each theme's Teaching Guide begins with an introductory welcome letter along with a week-by-week overview, ideas for integrating the Social-Emotional Focus, and specific tips for engaging families and community.

Welcome to the Theme

The Welcome to the Theme letter, written by one of our *Big Day for PreK* authors or consultants, introduces the four weeks ahead. Read the welcome letter before starting a theme to learn more about the theme topic and the underlying Big Idea that guides teaching and learning.

Welcome to the Theme letters

Theme Overview

The Theme Overview provides an at-a-glance snapshot of the four weeks of theme-based learning ahead. The Theme Overview includes key information, including:

- The theme's **Knowledge Focus.**
- The **Weekly Focus** for each theme week.
- The **Big Idea** that guides each week's learning.
- Key **concepts** for the week.
- Comprehensive weekly **theme vocabulary** lists.

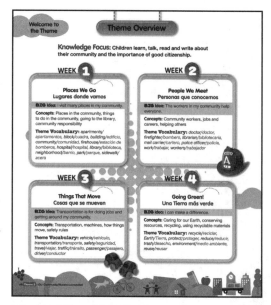

Theme 3 Teaching Guide

Social-Emotional Focus

It is important that PreK helps children develop **emotionally**, by becoming more aware of their own feelings and needs, as well as **socially**, by becoming more aware of the feelings and needs of others.

To support children's **social-emotional development,** each *Big Day for PreK* theme focuses on one of eight social-emotional areas reinforced throughout the theme: Cooperation, Kindness, Responsibility, Attention, Initiative, Self-Awareness, Curiosity, and Persistence.

The Social-Emotional Focus is integrated throughout your *Teaching Guide* lessons. The Social-Emotional Focus page at the start of each theme's *Teaching Guide* also includes additional support to help you reinforce the focus during informal learning times throughout the day.

Theme 3 Teaching Guide

Engaging Families and the Community

Big Day for PreK brings teachers, families, and the community together to support and extend children's learning. The suggestions in the Engaging Families and the Community pages at the start of each *Teaching Guide* provide ideas to involve families, plan field trips, and schedule classroom visitors.

Download a Spanish translation of these pages from Teacher Space to help you convey engagement suggestions to Spanish-speaking family members.

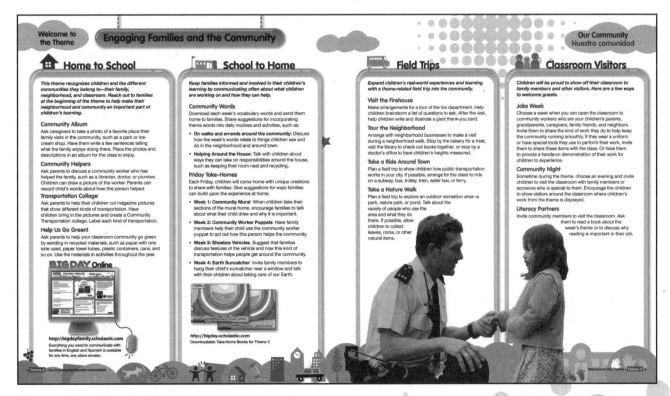

Theme 3 Teaching Guide

Preparing Learning Centers

Learning Centers provide interactive opportunities to extend learning each day with theme-specific activities.

Learning Centers At a Glance

Use Learning Centers At a Glance pages in the Learning Centers tab of your *Teaching Guides* as a quick reference to tailor each Center to extend theme learning. Learning Centers At a Glance pages include:

1 **Theme-Specific Learning Focus** Keep children engaged with the theme topic with focused activities in all eight Learning Centers.

2 **Audiobooks** Store audiobooks in the Reading & Listening Center so children can access theme Big Books while reading along in Little Books.

3 **Featured Pair on BookFlix** Identify the two BookFlix fiction-nonfiction Reading Pairs connected to the current theme.

4 **Books for All Centers** Add books from your own classroom or school library to support children's literacy in each Learning Center.

5 **ABC Place Suggestions** Look for activities that help reinforce alphabet knowledge in Learning Centers.

6 **Clifford Corner Ideas** Model and reinforce the theme's social-emotional focus with books and activities related to Clifford, the big red dog children know and love!

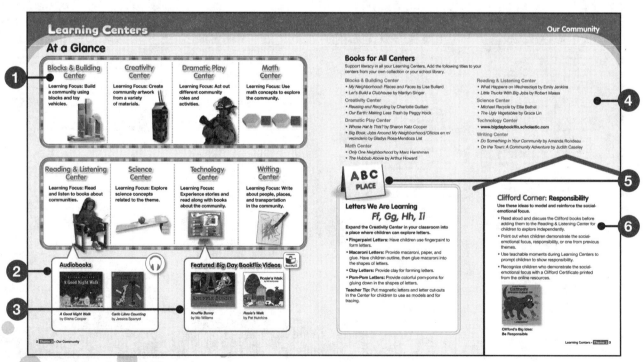

Theme 3 Teaching Guide

Setting Up Theme-Based Activities

Refer to the Learning Centers tab of your *Teaching Guides* for easy ideas to set up Centers that complement each week's learning. The Learning Centers tab includes materials checklists, suggested theme-related writing activities, and specific weekly activities for all eight Learning Centers: **Blocks & Building, Creativity, Dramatic Play, Math, Reading & Listening, Science, Technology,** and **Writing.**

Revisit the Learning Centers pages in your *Teaching Guides* to help you prepare activities for each week. For each Learning Center, you will find:

1 **Materials List** Make sure each Learning Center is equipped with all the materials needed for the month.

2 **Writing Connection Ideas** Make literacy part of every Learning Center with suggested writing activities.

3 **Week-by-Week Activities** Review week-by-week activities to engage children with the Weekly Focus.

4 **Learning Talk Language Support** Look for the "Learning Talk" feature for model language to help you reinforce oral language and social-emotional development when interacting with children in Learning Centers.

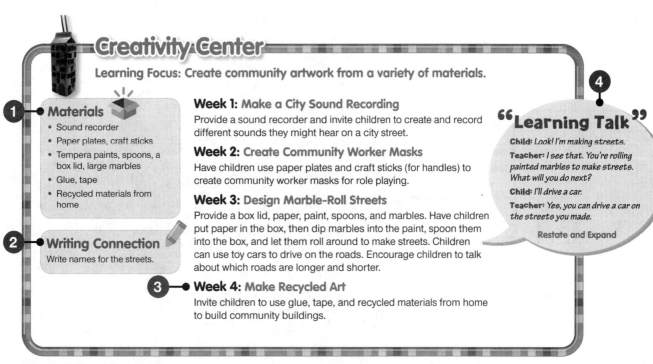

Creativity Center

Learning Focus: Create community artwork from a variety of materials.

1 **Materials**
- Sound recorder
- Paper plates, craft sticks
- Tempera paints, spoons, a box lid, large marbles
- Glue, tape
- Recycled materials from home

2 **Writing Connection**
Write names for the streets.

3

Week 1: Make a City Sound Recording
Provide a sound recorder and invite children to create and record different sounds they might hear on a city street.

Week 2: Create Community Worker Masks
Have children use paper plates and craft sticks (for handles) to create community worker masks for role playing.

Week 3: Design Marble-Roll Streets
Provide a box lid, paper, paint, spoons, and marbles. Have children put paper in the box, then dip marbles into the paint, spoon them into the box, and let them roll around to make streets. Children can use toy cars to drive on the roads. Encourage children to talk about which roads are longer and shorter.

Week 4: Make Recycled Art
Invite children to use glue, tape, and recycled materials from home to build community buildings.

4 **"Learning Talk"**

Child: *Look! I'm making streets.*
Teacher: *I see that. You're rolling painted marbles to make streets. What will you do next?*
Child: *I'll drive a car.*
Teacher: *Yes, you can drive a car on the streets you made.*

Restate and Expand

Theme 3 Teaching Guide

Planning a Week

Each theme includes four weeks of instruction. Weekly Overviews provide a snapshot of the key objectives taught in daily instruction as well as the literature selections you will enjoy reading and rereading to your young learners.

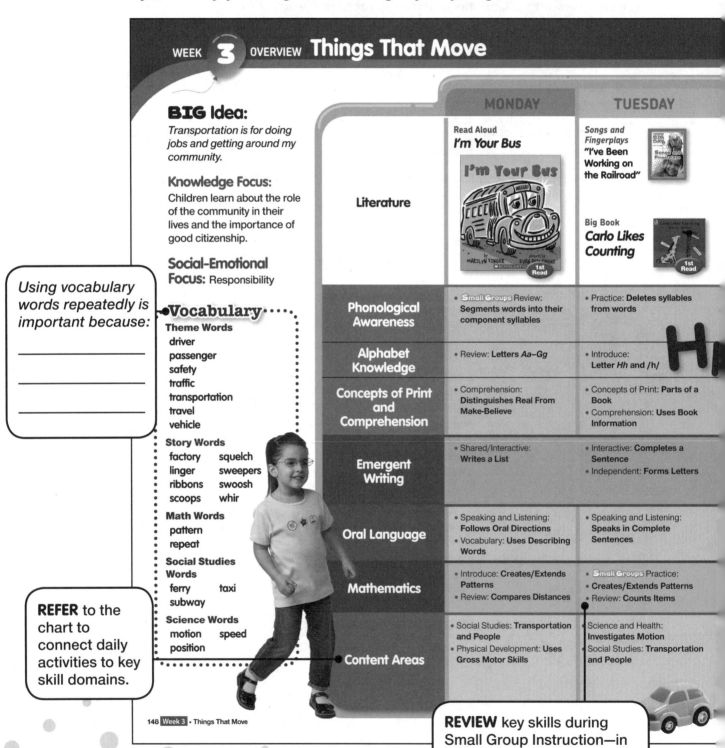

WEEK **3** OVERVIEW **Things That Move**

BIG Idea:
Transportation is for doing jobs and getting around my community.

Knowledge Focus:
Children learn about the role of the community in their lives and the importance of good citizenship.

Social-Emotional Focus: Responsibility

Using vocabulary words repeatedly is important because:
_____
_____
_____

Vocabulary

Theme Words
driver
passenger
safety
traffic
transportation
travel
vehicle

Story Words
factory   squelch
linger   sweepers
ribbons   swoosh
scoops   whir

Math Words
pattern
repeat

Social Studies Words
ferry   taxi
subway

Science Words
motion   speed
position

REFER to the chart to connect daily activities to key skill domains.

148 Week 3 · Things That Move

	MONDAY	TUESDAY
Literature	Read Aloud **I'm Your Bus** (1st Read)	Songs and Fingerplays "I've Been Working on the Railroad" Big Book **Carlo Likes Counting** (1st Read)
Phonological Awareness	• **Small Groups** Review: **Segments words into their component syllables**	• Practice: **Deletes syllables from words**
Alphabet Knowledge	• Review: **Letters** *Aa–Gg*	• Introduce: **Letter** *Hh* **and /h/**
Concepts of Print and Comprehension	• Comprehension: **Distinguishes Real From Make-Believe**	• Concepts of Print: **Parts of a Book** • Comprehension: **Uses Book Information**
Emergent Writing	• Shared/Interactive: **Writes a List**	• Interactive: **Completes a Sentence** • Independent: **Forms Letters**
Oral Language	• Speaking and Listening: **Follows Oral Directions** • Vocabulary: **Uses Describing Words**	• Speaking and Listening: **Speaks in Complete Sentences**
Mathematics	• Introduce: **Creates/Extends Patterns** • Review: **Compares Distances**	• **Small Groups** Practice: • **Creates/Extends Patterns** • Review: **Counts Items**
Content Areas	• Social Studies: **Transportation and People** • Physical Development: **Uses Gross Motor Skills**	• Science and Health: **Investigates Motion** • Social Studies: **Transportation and People**

Theme 3 Teaching Guide, Week 3

REVIEW key skills during Small Group Instruction—in emergent reading (Monday, Wednesday, and Friday) and math (Tuesday/Thursday).

> *One benefit of rereading books to children is:*
>
> _____
>
> _____
>
> _____

Our Community

WEDNESDAY	THURSDAY	FRIDAY
Read Aloud **Dig Dig Digging** *1st Read*	Songs and Fingerplays **"On the Go"** 	ABC Book **ABCDrive!**
Read Aloud **I'm Your Bus** *2nd Read*	Read Aloud **I'm Your Bus** *3rd Read* Read Aloud **Dig Dig Digging** *2nd Read*	 *2nd Read*
• **Small Groups** Practice: **Deletes syllables from words**	• Practice: **Deletes syllables from words**	• Practice: **Deletes syllables from words**
• Practice: **Letter Hh and /h/**	• Practice: **Letter Hh and /h/** • Review: **Letters Aa–Hh**	• **Small Groups** Practice/ Write/Assess: **Letter Hh**
• Comprehension: **Uses Picture Clues to Understand Words**	• Comprehension: **Retells a Story, Asks and Answers Questions, Uses Picture Clues**	• Comprehension: **Uses Book Information**
• Interactive: **Completes a Sentence**	• Independent: **Writes Symbols or Letters, Writes Name**	• Shared: **Contributes Ideas for Writing** • Independent: **Writes Symbols or Letters**
• Speaking and Listening: **Builds Oral Fluency** • Vocabulary: **Classifies Words Into Groups**	• Speaking and Listening: **Speaks Politely** • Vocabulary: **Understands Meanings of New Words**	• Speaking and Listening: **Responds Appropriately, Uses Longer Sentences**
• Practice: **Recognizes/ Creates/Extends Patterns**	• **Small Groups** Practice: **Recognizes/Creates/ Extends Patterns**	• Practice/Draw/Assess: **Creates Patterns**
• Social Studies: **Transportation and People** • Fine Arts: **Acts Out Stories** • Physical Development: **Uses Gross Motor Skills**	• Science and Health: **Investigates Motion** • Social Studies: **Transportation and People** • Physical Development: **Uses Fine Motor Skills**	• Science and Health: **Investigates Motion** • Social Studies: **Transportation and People** • Technology and Media: **Learns Through Technology**

BIG DAY Online

For Families

Remind families to share in their child's learning by exploring the *Big Day* Online **Family Space** for:

- *Big Day* BookFlix videos, multimedia books, and activities
- Tip of the Week
- Theme Letter
- Online Fun and Games
- Learn and Play Downloadables
- Family Resources and more!

AND Access the **Teacher Space** to customize lesson plans, get resources, set up family tips, and more.

> **UPDATE** messages and weekly tips on Family Space to build family engagement.

Learning Centers

Blocks & Building Center
- Use toy vehicles and blocks to "visit" places in the community.

Creativity Center
- Dip marbles in paint and let them roll to create streets for toy vehicles.

Dramatic Play Center
- Act out riding, driving, and getting on and off the bus.

Math Center
- Make AB patterns with vehicle sounds.

Reading & Listening Center
- Act out different types of vehicles from transportation books.

Science Center
- Explore how different vehicles roll down a ramp.

Technology Center
- Watch and read along with *Rosie's Walk*.

Writing Center
- Make and label a collaborative transportation collage.

> **ORGANIZE** materials needed for the week's Learning Center activities.

Planning a Day

Use the Day at a Glance summary to help you plan and prepare daily instruction for Circle and Story Time Big Experiences, Small Group Instruction, Small Group Intervention, and One-to-One Follow-Up.

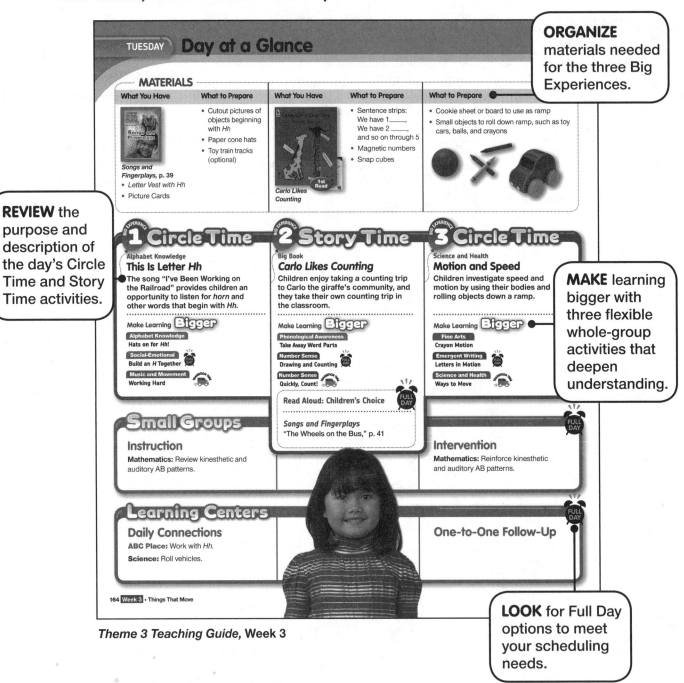

ORGANIZE materials needed for the three Big Experiences.

REVIEW the purpose and description of the day's Circle Time and Story Time activities.

MAKE learning bigger with three flexible whole-group activities that deepen understanding.

LOOK for Full Day options to meet your scheduling needs.

Theme 3 Teaching Guide, **Week 3**

Big Experiences

Each Big Day is organized around three 15–20-minute **Big Experiences**—during Circle Time or Story Time—that anchor conversation, play, and learning.

Each Big Experience is accompanied by three flexible 5–15-minute **Make Learning Bigger** activities, including a Full-Day option and Transition Time activity, that help reinforce and deepen learning while meeting your scheduling needs. Use the Transition Time activity each day to keep children engaged in learning as they move from one activity to the next. Then choose from the remaining options to support your schedule.

Each Big Experience includes an **Observe** feature to guide you in evaluating children's understanding of the skills and concepts that are most predictive of future school success. Each day concludes with suggestions for **One-to-One Follow-Up** linked to the day's observations to support children who could benefit from additional practice with key skills.

Small Group Instruction

Daily 10–20-minute **Small Group Instruction** activities build on concepts and solidify theme learning. Teaching small groups of three to five children helps you provide:

- Additional guidance and practice with skills
- Targeted, individualized support
- Immediate feedback

Each Small Group Instruction lesson includes an **Observe** feature to help you determine whether children are meeting learning goals and a **Small Group Intervention** activity to provide additional practice and support as needed.

Learning Centers

Learning Centers extend concepts introduced during Big Experiences and provide children with opportunities for intentional play and independent exploration. Children learn to work independently and collaboratively as they engage in theme-specific activities in any of the eight Learning Centers.

Observe children as they participate in Learning Center activities. Look for opportunities to have meaningful conversations with children and make connections to theme content.

Big Hint

Observing children in Learning Centers is a great way to learn more about individual interests and developmental progress.

Teaching Circle Time Big Experiences

Gather children together to engage in whole-group integrated learning experiences on topics such as sound patterns or motion and speed that serve as a springboard for learning throughout the day.

LOOK for color-coded learning objectives to see the cross-curricular connections at a glance.

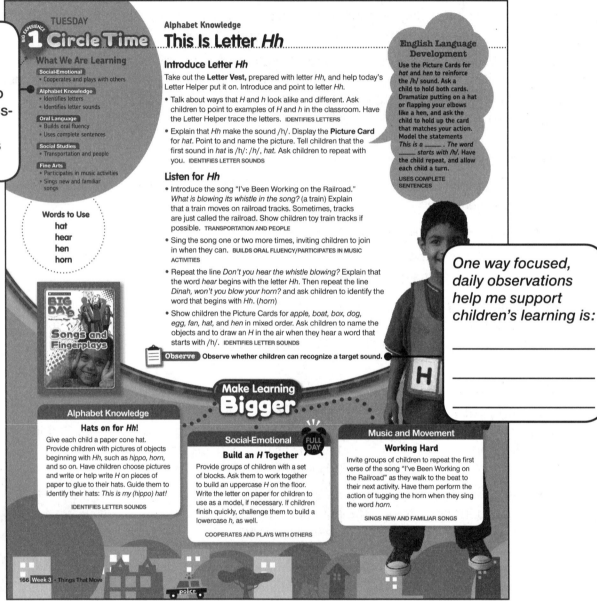

Theme 3 Teaching Guide, Week 3

Reflection: Circle Time

Use the prompts below to guide your reflection on the Circle Time experience.

1 *Big Day for PreK* provides integrated learning experiences. Look at the Circle Time learning objectives. How are the **five learning domains** integrated into this Big Experience?

_____

_____

_____

2 Each Big Experience includes an **Observe** to help you monitor children's understanding of essential skills and behaviors. What skill are you observing during this Circle Time activity?

_____

_____

_____

3 Look for the **English Language Development** (or **Bridge to English** in Spanish lessons) feature for point-of-use suggestions for explicit language instruction. How does the **English Language Development** feature for this Circle Time experience support children's understanding of letter *Hh?*

_____

_____

_____

4 What is one thing you find engaging in this Circle Time lesson?

_____

_____

_____

BIG TRAINING 1 EXPERIENCE

Teaching Story Time Big Experiences

Make Story Time an interactive learning experience by engaging children in dialogue as they read and explore a theme-related story.

BUILD children's oral language skills with the English Language Development suggestions.

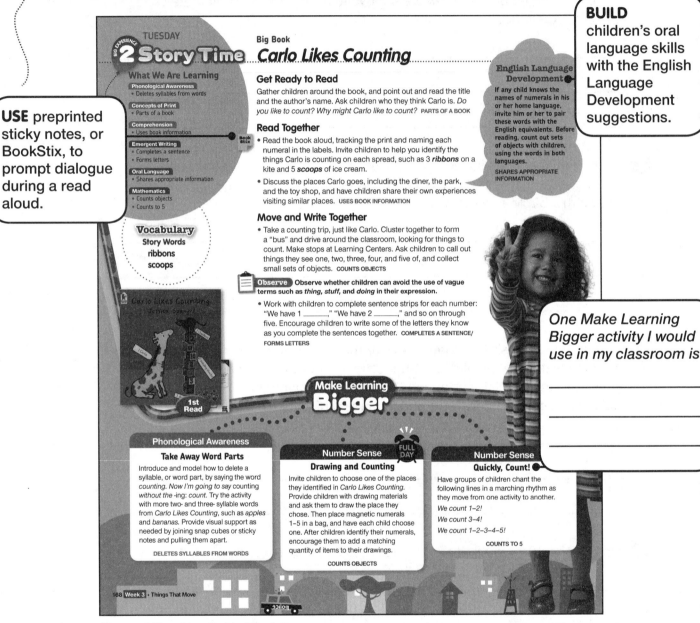

USE preprinted sticky notes, or BookStix, to prompt dialogue during a read aloud.

TUESDAY

BIG EXPERIENCE 2 Story Time

What We Are Learning

Phonological Awareness
- Deletes syllables from words

Concepts of Print
- Parts of a book

Comprehension
- Uses book information

Emergent Writing
- Completes a sentence
- Forms letters

Oral Language
- Shares appropriate information

Mathematics
- Counts objects
- Counts to 5

Vocabulary
Story Words
ribbons
scoops

1st Read

Big Book
Carlo Likes Counting

Get Ready to Read
Gather children around the book, and point out and read the title and the author's name. Ask children who they think Carlo is. *Do you like to count? Why might Carlo like to count?* PARTS OF A BOOK

Read Together
Book Stix
- Read the book aloud, tracking the print and naming each numeral in the labels. Invite children to help you identify the things Carlo is counting on each spread, such as 3 ***ribbons*** on a kite and 5 ***scoops*** of ice cream.
- Discuss the places Carlo goes, including the diner, the park, and the toy shop, and have children share their own experiences visiting similar places. USES BOOK INFORMATION

English Language Development
If any child knows the names of numerals in his or her home language, invite him or her to pair these words with the English equivalents. Before reading, count out sets of objects with children, using the words in both languages.
SHARES APPROPRIATE INFORMATION

Move and Write Together
- Take a counting trip, just like Carlo. Cluster together to form a "bus" and drive around the classroom, looking for things to count. Make stops at Learning Centers. Ask children to call out things they see one, two, three, four, and five of, and collect small sets of objects. COUNTS OBJECTS

Observe **Observe whether children can avoid the use of vague terms such as *thing, stuff,* and *doing* in their expression.**

- Work with children to complete sentence strips for each number: "We have 1 ______," "We have 2 ______," and so on through five. Encourage children to write some of the letters they know as you complete the sentences together. COMPLETES A SENTENCE/ FORMS LETTERS

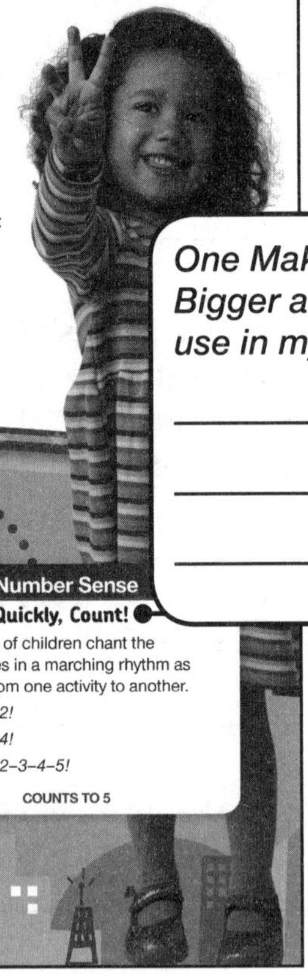

One Make Learning Bigger activity I would use in my classroom is

____

____

____

Make Learning Bigger

Phonological Awareness
Take Away Word Parts
Introduce and model how to delete a syllable, or word part, by saying the word *counting. Now I'm going to say* counting *without the -ing: count.* Try the activity with more two- and three- syllable words from *Carlo Likes Counting*, such as *apples* and *bananas*. Provide visual support as needed by joining snap cubes or sticky notes and pulling them apart.
DELETES SYLLABLES FROM WORDS

Number Sense FULL DAY
Drawing and Counting
Invite children to choose one of the places they identified in *Carlo Likes Counting*. Provide children with drawing materials and ask them to draw the place they chose. Then place magnetic numerals 1–5 in a bag, and have each child choose one. After children identify their numerals, encourage them to add a matching quantity of items to their drawings.
COUNTS OBJECTS

Number Sense
Quickly, Count!
Have groups of children chant the following lines in a marching rhythm as they move from one activity to another.
We count 1–2!
We count 3–4!
We count 1–2–3–4–5!
COUNTS TO 5

168 Week 3 • Things That Move

Theme 3 Teaching Guide, Week 3

Reflect: Story Time

Use the prompts below to guide your reflection on the Story Time experience.

1 *Big Day for PreK* Read Aloud, Shared Reading, and Alphabet Books are paired with preprinted sticky notes, or **BookStix**, that provide prompts to engage children in book discussions. What is one benefit of using BookStix to make Story Time interactive?

_____

_____

_____

_____

BookStix

2 BookStix include prompts to use during the **first reading** of a book as well as prompts for repeated readings. During this Story Time experience, you read *Carlo Likes Counting* together for the first time. How might you **introduce** the book to get children ready to read?

_____

_____

_____

3 Each Big Experience includes an **Observe** feature to help you monitor children's understanding of a specific skill. What skill are you observing during this Story Time activity?

_____

_____

_____

4 What is one aspect of this Story Time lesson that you are excited to try?

_____

_____

_____

Building Language and Literacy

BIG TRAINING 3 EXPERIENCE

In a literacy-rich Big Day for PreK *classroom, each day provides multiple opportunities for children to build and strengthen their reading and language skills.*

Books, Books, and More Books!

Big Day for PreK surrounds children with a variety of books (available in English and Spanish) to support theme learning in and out of the classroom. Refer to the chart below for an overview of the types of books included in *Big Day for PreK*.

Book Type	Description	When to Use
Alphabet Books	8 books (1 per theme) for developing alphabet knowledge, each with BookStix sticky notes	During **Story Time** or **Children's Choice** full-day read aloud option
Big Books, Little Books, Audiobooks	16 Big Books (2 per theme), each with BookStix sticky notes, audiobooks, and 4 copies of Little Book versions to make accessible in the Reading & Listening Center	During **Story Time** or in **Learning Centers** (Reading & Listening Center)
Read Aloud Books	64 books (8 per theme) related to theme learning, each with BookStix sticky notes	During **Story Time**
Clifford Books	10 books to guide social-emotional development, featuring Clifford, the lovable big red dog	To reinforce the theme's social-emotional focus during **Circle Time, Children's Choice,** or in **Learning Centers** (Reading & Listening Center)
BookFlix Books Online	16 fiction-nonfiction Reading Pairs, two pairs per *Big Day for PreK* theme	During **Learning Centers** (Technology Center), **Story Time**, or the **Children's Choice** full-day read aloud option; **anywhere, anytime,** from any computer with an Internet connection
Downloadable Books	Downloadable Theme Books, Alphabet Mini-books, and Take-Home Books on Teacher Space and Family Space for families and children to read together at home	**Anytime!**

Big Hint

See *Professional Handbook* pages xx–xxi for a comprehensive list of theme-specific *Big Day for PreK* book titles for each book type.

Dialogic Reading

Big Day for PreK uses a dialogic reading approach to engage children actively during read alouds. Dialogic reading makes reading books an interactive learning experience that enhances children's language and literacy skills through questions and prompts. During a read aloud, follow the PEER sequence to increase attention and engagement, deepen comprehension, and build vocabulary:

Prompt children to say something about the book (e.g., while pointing to an image of a bear, ask *What is this?*).

Evaluate the response (e.g., when the child says, *Bear!*, respond with *Yes! It is a bear!*).

Expand on the response by rephrasing and adding to it (e.g., *It's a big, brown bear!*).

Repeat the prompt to check understanding and give children additional opportunities for using language (e.g., *Can you say "big, brown bear?"*).

Reading Beyond the Book With BookStix

Your *Teaching Guides* provide support to help you make Story Time an interactive learning experience. Each Big Book and Read Aloud Book comes with a preprinted BookStix sticky note that you can attach to the back of your book cover. BookStix use CROWD prompts to engage children in conversation:

Completion Prompt children to complete a sentence (e.g., *When the mouse ran right by the lion, the lion _____ .*).

Recall Ask about what happened to help children comprehend and describe book events (e.g., *How did the mouse help the lion?*).

Open-ended Ask open-ended questions based on illustrations to help children attend to details and develop ideas (e.g., *What is happening in this picture?*).

Wh- prompts Ask *who*, *what*, *where*, *when*, and *why* questions to focus on vocabulary and story events (e.g., *What is this called?*).

Distancing Guide children to relate pictures or events to their lives and experience (e.g., *What does it feel like when you help a friend?*).

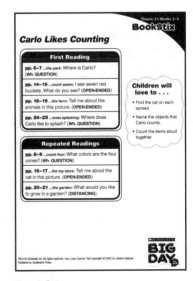

BookStix

Teaching With Responsive Instruction

Each daily lesson includes ideas for modifying Big Experiences, teaching children in small groups, and providing one-to-one support.

One modification I would use to support children during Big Experiences is . . .

_____

_____

_____

USE the Observe feature embedded in daily Big Experience lessons to provide one-to-one support.

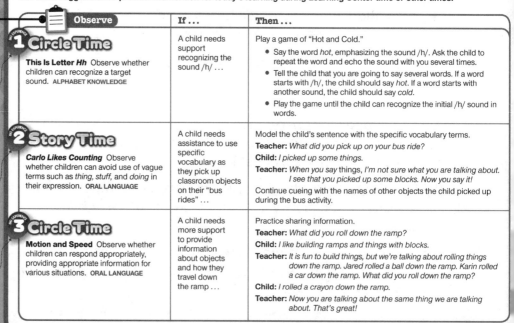

TUESDAY **Responsive Instruction**

Modifications

Use these suggestions to differentiate instruction to meet individual needs.

3-Year-Olds

This Is Letter *Hh* Help children practice the /h/ sound by having them take a deep breath and then repeat the sound several times in a row. Suggest that /h/ can sound like laughing: *Ha, ha, ha!*

Special Needs

Motion and Speed If a child has trouble waiting his or her turn in the ramp activity, give him or her a "special" job to engage in. For example, he or she may collect objects at the bottom of the ramp or be appointed as "starter" to tell others when to let their object go.

Enrichment

Carlo Likes Counting Encourage children to work together to draw a simple picture graph to chart the objects that children counted on their bus ride around the room.

One-to-One Follow-Up

Use these suggestions to provide intervention for today's learning during Learning Center time or other times.

Observe	If . . .	Then . . .
1 Circle Time **This Is Letter *Hh*** Observe whether children can recognize a target sound. ALPHABET KNOWLEDGE	A child needs support recognizing the sound /h/ . . .	Play a game of "Hot and Cold." • Say the word *hot*, emphasizing the sound /h/. Ask the child to repeat the word and echo the sound with you several times. • Tell the child that you are going to say several words. If a word starts with /h/, the child should say *hot*. If a word starts with another sound, the child should say *cold*. • Play the game until the child can recognize the initial /h/ sound in words.
2 Story Time ***Carlo Likes Counting*** Observe whether children can avoid use of vague terms such as *thing, stuff,* and *doing* in their expression. ORAL LANGUAGE	A child needs assistance to use specific vocabulary as they pick up classroom objects on their "bus rides" . . .	Model the child's sentence with the specific vocabulary terms. **Teacher:** *What did you pick up on your bus ride?* **Child:** *I picked up some things.* **Teacher:** *When you say things, I'm not sure what you are talking about. I see that you picked up some blocks. Now you say it!* Continue cueing with the names of other objects the child picked up during the bus activity.
3 Circle Time **Motion and Speed** Observe whether children can respond appropriately, providing appropriate information for various situations. ORAL LANGUAGE	A child needs more support to provide information about objects and how they travel down the ramp . . .	Practice sharing information. **Teacher:** *What did you roll down the ramp?* **Child:** *I like building ramps and things with blocks.* **Teacher:** *It is fun to build things, but we're talking about rolling things down the ramp. Jared rolled a ball down the ramp. Karin rolled a car down the ramp. What did you roll down the ramp?* **Child:** *I rolled a crayon down the ramp.* **Teacher:** *Now you are talking about the same thing we are talking about. That's great!*

Theme 3 Teaching Guide, Week 3

Small Groups Instruction

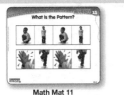

MATERIALS

What You Have

Math Mat 11

What To Prepare

🖊 Copies of downloadable Math Mat 11

Mathematics

Mimic, Recognize, and Extend Kinesthetic and Auditory AB Patterns

Review

Display **Math Mat 11** and review the pattern in the first row. Ask children to help you discover the pattern. *This is a pattern of two motions, repeated over and over. What happens first?* (crouch down) *Next?* (stand up) *Let's repeat it.*

Model

Turn to Math Mat, Side B. Ask what the child is doing in each of the pictures in the first row. Point to the first empty box and ask *What do you think this boy will do next?* (crouch) *What will he do after that?* (stand) Have children repeat the AB pattern.

Practice

Have children work in small groups to act out and complete the pattern in the second row. Ask individuals to lead others, calling out *clap, stomp, clap, stomp.*

Observe	If ...	Then ...
Observe whether children can recognize, extend, and create an auditory or kinesthetic AB pattern.	A child does not recognize, extend, and create patterns accurately ...	Demonstrate a few patterns and non-patterns, asking *Is this a pattern?* If the answer is *no*, ask the child to make your actions into a pattern. Use both sound and motion patterns as needed. See additional reinforcement below.

Small Groups Intervention

MATERIALS

What To Prepare

🖊 Copies of downloadable Math Mat 11

FULL DAY

Reinforce

If children demonstrate the need for additional practice with mimicking, recognizing, and extending kinesthetic and auditory AB patterns, explain and demonstrate some everyday patterns, such as nodding your head up and down and the *whee-eww, whee-eww* sound of a siren. Remind children that patterns repeat over and over again.

Practice

Demonstrate a simple kinesthetic pattern, such as raising and lowering your arms. Ask children to continue the pattern. Provide copies of the **downloadable Math Mat 11.** Point to the pictures and have children perform the actions: crouch, stand, crouch, stand. Ask children to continue the pattern. Repeat with other movement patterns.

PROVIDE small groups with direct instruction in literacy (Mondays, Wednesdays, and Fridays) and math skills (Tuesdays and Thursdays).

USE the Observe feature to plan targeted instruction.

USE Small Group Intervention for those who might benefit from further review and practice.

Modifying Big Experiences

Each daily lesson includes ideas for modifying whole-group Big Experience activities to meet children's individual needs.

English Language Learners

Children may enter prekindergarten with diverse linguistic backgrounds and varying experiences with the English language. For children whose families speak languages other than English, explicit English language instruction is especially beneficial.

Use the English Language Development suggestions that appear in Circle Time and Story Time activities in your *Teaching Guides* to provide English learners and *all* young learners with explicit language instruction. If teaching children in Spanish, look for the Bridge to English feature to make connections to English.

Children With Special Needs

Children with special needs may need additional scaffolding or a different approach to instruction (e.g., visual aids, manipulatives, oral directions). Look to the Responsive Instruction pages at the end of each daily lesson in the *Teaching Guides* for help modifying daily Circle Time and Story Time activities to meet children's individual needs.

3-Year-Olds

3-year-old children are bursting with energy and curiosity—and eager to test their independence. Though they may be eager and willing to fully participate in all classroom activities, 3-year-olds are at different points in their language, literacy, social-emotional, and physical development than their 4-year-old classmates. If you are teaching a multiage classroom, refer to the modifications suggested in the Responsive Instruction pages in your *Teaching Guides* to tailor daily Story Time and Circle Time activities to meet the developmental needs of the 3-year-olds in your classroom.

Enrichment

Going to school is especially exciting for young learners! Encourage their natural curiosity and interest in learning with the Enrichment suggestions in the Responsive Instruction pages of your *Teaching Guides* to extend and deepen learning experiences.

English Language Development

Explain the word *favorite* to children with some simple demonstrations. Pick up a toy, make a face that shows indifference or dislike, and say *This* is not *my favorite toy.* Then pick up another toy, show happiness, hug the toy, and say *This is my favorite toy.* Then have children demonstrate their own favorites.

UNDERSTANDS MEANINGS OF NEW WORDS

Big Hint

See *Professional Handbook* pages 56–61 for more on modifying Big Experiences, Small Group Instruction, and Learning Centers to meet individual needs.

Planning Small Group Instruction

Daily Small Group Instruction activities provide children with additional teacher guidance and support with key literacy and math skills during Learning Center time.

Targeted Small Group Instruction

Working with a small group of 3–5 children provides you with an opportunity to break down instruction into smaller, more manageable steps, give children additional support, and offer immediate feedback.

Your *Big Day for PreK Teaching Guides* include daily Small Group Instruction activities to support children with literacy skills (on Mondays, Wednesdays, and Fridays) and mathematics skills (on Tuesdays and Thursdays). Each Small Group Instruction lesson includes a list of materials to help you prepare; directions for introducing or reviewing, modeling, and practicing the skill; and an Observe to focus your observations and target instruction.

Making Time for Small Groups

You can easily include the 10–20-minute Small Group Instruction activity in a half- or full-day schedule with small-group rotations during Learning Center time. Follow these simple steps to make Small Group Instruction a successful part of the day:

1. Form heterogeneous groups of 3–5 children in advance.

2. Create a chart or display to help children know their group assignment (e.g., hang four sheets of colored paper with children's names on them, then call out "green" when you're ready to work with the "green" group).

3. Help children find their group (e.g., locating their photograph and name on the "green" paper).

4. Introduce a signal (e.g., music, whistle, bell) to help children recognize when it's time to go to the Small Group Instruction table during scheduled Learning Center time.

5. Call the first group to the Small Group Instruction table at the start of Learning Center time. Then use the signal to indicate when you are ready for the next group!

Big Hint

Practice makes perfect! When introducing small-group rotations for the first time, have children practice, practice, practice the procedure beforehand.

Observing Children's Progress

Each Small Group Instruction activity includes an Observe feature to guide you to monitor children's understanding of the targeted skill. Download and print the **Small Group Observation Guide** from Teacher Space. Then use the guide to note which children demonstrate an understanding of the skill and which children could use additional support. Use the suggestions in the Observe feature to provide point-of-use support or plan Small Group Intervention.

Observe	If . . .	Then . . .
Observe whether children can recognize, extend, and create an auditory or kinesthetic AB pattern.	A child does not recognize, extend, and create patterns accurately . . .	Demonstrate a few patterns and non-patterns, asking *Is this a pattern?* If the answer is *no*, ask the child to make your actions into a pattern. Use both sound and motion patterns as needed. See additional reinforcement below.

Theme 3 Teaching Guide, Week 3, Tuesday

Planning Small Group Intervention

Each Small Group Instruction lesson includes a Small Group Intervention activity to support children who could benefit from additional review or practice. Small Group Intervention can easily take place during the afternoon Learning Center time for a full-day schedule. If providing intervention within a half-day schedule, consider the following suggestions:

- Teach the Small Group Intervention activity one-to-one during Learning Centers.

- Have Small Group Instruction rotations for the first 40 minutes of Learning Center time, then spend the last 10–20 minutes having a select group return for Small Group Intervention.

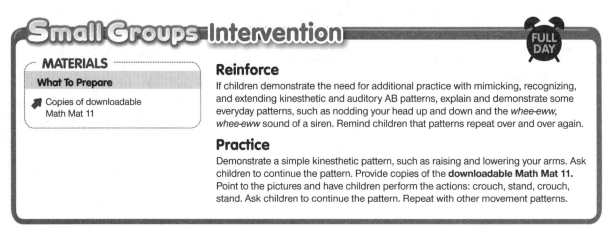

Small Groups Intervention

FULL DAY

MATERIALS

What To Prepare

🔖 Copies of downloadable Math Mat 11

Reinforce

If children demonstrate the need for additional practice with mimicking, recognizing, and extending kinesthetic and auditory AB patterns, explain and demonstrate some everyday patterns, such as nodding your head up and down and the *whee-eww, whee-eww* sound of a siren. Remind children that patterns repeat over and over again.

Practice

Demonstrate a simple kinesthetic pattern, such as raising and lowering your arms. Ask children to continue the pattern. Provide copies of the **downloadable Math Mat 11.** Point to the pictures and have children perform the actions: crouch, stand, crouch, stand. Ask children to continue the pattern. Repeat with other movement patterns.

Theme 3 Teaching Guide, Week 3, Tuesday

Supporting Learners One-to-One

All children can benefit from even a few minutes of individual attention each day.

Supporting One Child at a Time

While it may seem overwhelming to think about spending quality one-to-one time with children during the day, research has shown that even a few well-timed minutes with a child can be worthwhile. The nature of one-to-one time depends on each child and his or her individual needs. *Big Day for PreK* helps you identify these needs through a combination of daily teacher observations and responsive instruction.

Targeting Support

Big Day for PreK provides a simple road map for making focused, daily classroom observations and planning follow-up support.

> **Step 1** Use the **Observe** feature that appears in your *Teaching Guide* lessons to monitor children's understanding of key skills.

> **Step 2** Download and print the **Circle Time/Story Time Observation Guide** for the current theme week from Teacher Space. Record names of children who demonstrate understanding of the skill and those who could use additional practice and review.

> **Step 3** Use the **One-to-One Follow-Up** suggestions in the Responsive Instruction pages in your *Teaching Guides* to individualize support.

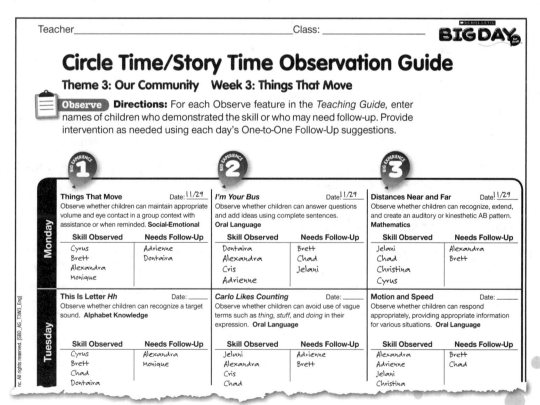

Circle Time/Story Time Observation Guide, Theme 3, Week 3

Providing One-to-One Follow-Up

After recording observations on the Circle Time/Story Time Observation Guide, refer to the One-to-One Follow-Up chart on the Responsive Instruction pages of your *Teaching Guides*. Check the "If" statements to identify specific areas of development. If a child requires additional support, use the "Then" suggestions to reinforce the skill using new content and, when appropriate, a different approach.

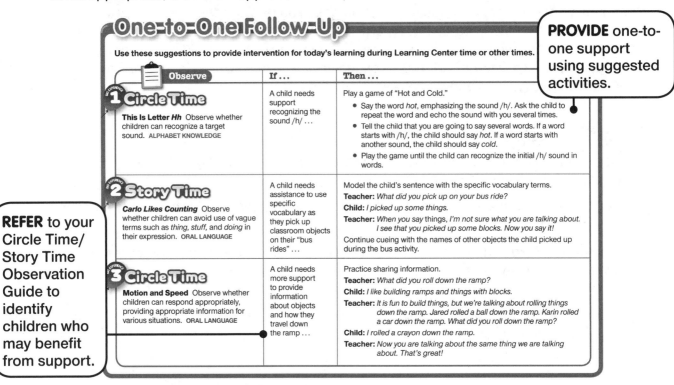

PROVIDE one-to-one support using suggested activities.

REFER to your Circle Time/ Story Time Observation Guide to identify children who may benefit from support.

One-to-One Follow-Up

Use these suggestions to provide intervention for today's learning during Learning Center time or other times.

Observe	If...	Then...
1 Circle Time **This Is Letter *Hh*** Observe whether children can recognize a target sound. ALPHABET KNOWLEDGE	A child needs support recognizing the sound /h/ ...	Play a game of "Hot and Cold." • Say the word *hot*, emphasizing the sound /h/. Ask the child to repeat the word and echo the sound with you several times. • Tell the child that you are going to say several words. If a word starts with /h/, the child should say *hot*. If a word starts with another sound, the child should say *cold*. • Play the game until the child can recognize the initial /h/ sound in words.
2 Story Time **Carlo Likes Counting** Observe whether children can avoid use of vague terms such as *thing, stuff,* and *doing* in their expression. ORAL LANGUAGE	A child needs assistance to use specific vocabulary as they pick up classroom objects on their "bus rides" ...	Model the child's sentence with the specific vocabulary terms. **Teacher:** *What did you pick up on your bus ride?* **Child:** *I picked up some things.* **Teacher:** *When you say things, I'm not sure what you are talking about. I see that you picked up some blocks. Now you say it!* Continue cueing with the names of other objects the child picked up during the bus activity.
3 Circle Time **Motion and Speed** Observe whether children can respond appropriately, providing appropriate information for various situations. ORAL LANGUAGE	A child needs more support to provide information about objects and how they travel down the ramp ...	Practice sharing information. **Teacher:** *What did you roll down the ramp?* **Child:** *I like building ramps and things with blocks.* **Teacher:** *It is fun to build things, but we're talking about rolling things down the ramp. Jared rolled a ball down the ramp. Karin rolled a car down the ramp. What did you roll down the ramp?* **Child:** *I rolled a crayon down the ramp.* **Teacher:** *Now you are talking about the same thing we are talking about. That's great!*

Theme 3 Teaching Guide, **Week 3, Tuesday**

Making Time for One-to-One

Each One-to-One Follow-Up activity only takes 2 or 3 minutes, so you can easily fit it into your day! Consider the following suggestions to make time for one-to-one support.

- Provide one-to-one instruction in the last 10–20 minutes of Learning Center time. Visit children as they play in the Centers.

- Have an aide meet with children for Small Group Instruction, while you provide individual children with one-to-one support.

- Engage a child in conversation or make a game of the targeted skill during outside time. For example, model an AB movement pattern (e.g., jump, step, jump, step) and have the child mimic the movement. Then ask him or her to create an AB movement pattern for you to mimic.

Preparing Your Classroom

Getting Your Classroom Ready

It's time to get ready for the big year ahead! Create a safe, positive, and orderly environment that will engage all children in learning.

Arranging the Classroom Layout

Preparing your classroom for a big year with *Big Day for PreK* means creating areas for whole-group Big Experiences, Small Group Instruction, and Learning Centers. Consider the general tips below and refer to **pages 43–49** to guide you in arranging the classroom to meet your daily needs.

- Divide the space into active and quiet areas.
- Use low, child-friendly furniture to define each space.
- Make sure children are visible when standing in any area of the room.
- Provide a personalized space for children to store belongings.
- Label key areas of the room, such as Learning Centers, Small Group Instruction table, and the whole-group meeting area.
- Organize children's materials in clearly labeled, easily accessible bins, cabinets, shelves, etc.

Creating a Schedule

A clear and consistent schedule provides children with a sense of security. Knowing what's ahead helps the day go more smoothly—for children and adults alike! Turn to **pages 50–52** to help you schedule your day.

Managing the Day

Young learners are often excited and eager to learn! Help focus children's enthusiasm for a productive day! Refer to **pages 53–60** for tips on establishing routines, managing Learning Centers, and working with small groups.

Setting Up Learning Centers

Learning Centers provide an opportunity for children to explore their interests, make individual choices, and work collaboratively.

Arranging the Space

Read the descriptions and requirements for each Center to guide you as you set up your room. Place a star next to Centers that might be noisy, such as the Dramatic Play Center, as a reminder to keep these areas separate from quieter Learning Centers.

Learning Center	Description	Requirements
Blocks & Building	Build structures using blocks of various shapes, sizes, colors.	• Spacious area, removed from quieter Centers • Low, open shelves to store blocks
Creativity	Use various materials to draw, create collages, paint, sculpt, etc.	• Storage for supplies (e.g., cabinet, shelves) • Table and chairs, easels • Easy-to-clean flooring and sink for cleanup • Space for artwork to dry
Dramatic Play	Act out theme-related scenarios.	• Child-size furniture • Storage for props (e.g., trunk, cabinet)
Math	Use manipulatives to explore quantity, size, shapes, and numerals.	• Storage for manipulatives (e.g., bins) • Table and chairs
Reading & Listening	Read books and/or listen to audiobooks independently.	• Bookshelves and comfortable child-size seating (e.g., bean bags) • Headphones and CD player
Science	Experiment, observe, and conduct investigations.	• Spacious area • Natural light • Table and chairs
Technology	Use computers to explore BookFlix or age-appropriate software.	• Computers with Internet connection • Headphones • Electrical outlets • Table and chairs
Writing	Write letters, respond to prompts, make books, etc. using a variety of materials.	• Storage for materials (e.g., trays, boxes) • Table and chairs

Gathering and Organizing Materials

Once you have arranged each space, the next step is to stock Learning Centers with the necessary supplies. Use clearly labeled bins, jars, boxes, plastic storage containers, cabinets, and bookshelves to keep materials organized. Refer to the materials checklist below as you prepare each Center.

Blocks & Building Center

❑ A variety of blocks, organized and labeled by type, size, shape

❑ Theme-related props (e.g., miniature vehicles, toy figures)

Creativity Center

❑ A variety of paper (e.g., colored construction paper, tissue paper)

❑ A variety of drawing and painting materials (e.g., brushes, sponges, stencils, chalk, paint, crayons)

❑ Adhesive (e.g., glue sticks, white glue, tape)

❑ Age-appropriate scissors

❑ Paper punches

❑ Plastic egg cartons or palettes for paint

❑ Play dough or clay for sculpting

❑ Embellishments (e.g., feathers, buttons, ribbons)

❑ Child-size easels

Dramatic Play Center

❑ Child-size furniture (e.g., kitchen table)

❑ Authentic props (e.g., food containers, silverware, dishes, magazines, suitcases, dress-up clothes)

❑ Unbreakable floor-length mirror

❑ Theme-related props (e.g., miniature vehicles, toy figures)

Math Center

❑ Manipulatives from the *Big Day for PreK* Manipulatives Kit (e.g., **Number Cards, Pattern Blocks, Attribute Blocks, Counting Bears, Snap Cubes**)

❑ A variety of templates for recording information (e.g., graphs, charts)

❑ Posters with numbers and geometric shapes (e.g., **Math Mats**) displayed at eye level

Big Hint

Introduce Learning Centers gradually. Stock each Center with basic supplies, adding more as children become more comfortable.

Reading & Listening Center

- ❑ Comfortable seating (e.g. soft rug, giant floor pillows, beanbag chairs)
- ❑ Variety of books, including **Clifford books** and the **Little Book** versions of Big Books read during Story Time
- ❑ Audiobooks and listening equipment (e.g., CD player, MP3 player)
- ❑ Headphones

Science Center

- ❑ Materials for growing plants (e.g., cups, seeds, soil)
- ❑ Discovery trays (e.g., magnet with sampling of metal and nonmetal objects)
- ❑ **Jumbo Magnifiers** from the *Big Day for PreK* Manipulatives Kit
- ❑ Measuring supplies (e.g., rulers, containers, measuring cups)
- ❑ **Balance** from the *Big Day for PreK* Manipulatives Kit and objects to compare weight (e.g., feathers, marbles)
- ❑ **Magnetic Healthy Food Kit** from the *Big Day for PreK* Manipulatives Kit
- ❑ Supplies to record data (e.g., clipboards, charts, pencils)
- ❑ Theme-related **Science Posters** displayed at eye level

Technology Center

- ❑ Computers with Internet connection
- ❑ Headsets and hooks to store them

Writing Center

- ❑ Dry-erase boards, felt boards, and **Magnetic Boards** with storytelling figures and letters
- ❑ Picture dictionaries
- ❑ **Letter Cards**
- ❑ Writing utensils (e.g., crayons, pencils, markers)
- ❑ Variety of paper (e.g., construction, lined)
- ❑ Book-binding materials (e.g., tape, glue, hole-punches, twist ties, staplers)
- ❑ **Alphabet Frieze** poster displayed nearby
- ❑ **Vocabulary cutouts**, downloadable from Teacher Space, to create theme Word Walls

Big Hint

Refer to the Learning Centers tab of your *Teaching Guides* for tips on integrating reading and writing in every Center!

Creating a Safe Environment

Young learners are curious and eager to explore. Take precautions to ensure that children can explore and interact with their environment safely.

Safety Checklist

When it comes to young children, safety is incredibly important! Before your young explorers come through the door, make sure your classroom is safe and child-friendly!

Physical Space

- ❏ Use low bookshelves to create well-defined spaces.
- ❏ Arrange the space to create walkways, rather than runways.
- ❏ Use age-appropriate furniture (e.g., child-size tables and chairs)
- ❏ Check furniture regularly for splinters, loose screws, etc.
- ❏ Anchor wobbly or top-heavy furniture to walls to prevent toppling.
- ❏ Secure rugs with Velcro or nonslip backing to prevent tripping.
- ❏ Check to make sure all children's work and play areas are visible to you at all times.
- ❏ _____
  _____

Classroom Materials

- ❏ Make sure all materials are age-appropriate (e.g., nontoxic, no sharp edges, no choking hazards).
- ❏ Prevent tripping hazards by keeping materials well-organized in clearly labeled bins or shelves.
- ❏ Clean and sanitize materials daily to reduce the spread of germs.
- ❏ _____
  _____

Big Hint

Visit the U.S. Consumer Product Safety Commission website **http://www.cpsc.gov** monthly to check for safety recalls.

Classroom Environment

- ❏ Cover unused electrical outlets.
- ❏ Keep traffic areas free of cords and small objects.
- ❏ Store cleaning supplies or sharp objects in locked cabinets.
- ❏ Check that fire extinguishers and smoke detectors are in place and work properly.
- ❏ _____
  _____

Daily Cleanup Procedure

Keeping your classroom clean and well-organized is an important part of maintaining a safe learning environment. Introduce a daily cleanup procedure to get children involved in the process. Not only will children learn about classroom safety, but they will also get extra practice with skills such as sorting and classifying, following directions, and working collaboratively!

Work with a partner or independently to come up with a cleanup procedure that you might try in your classroom. For example, steps might include:

1 Listen for the signal (e.g., bell, music, whistle).

2 Stop what you're doing.

3 Wait for directions.

4 Store materials.

5 Return to meeting area.

Our Cleanup Procedure

Big Hint

Assign a child to be a Classroom Cleanup Announcer, responsible for giving the cleanup signal at the end of Learning Center time.

Arranging the Classroom

Organizing and arranging your classroom is key to effectively managing your day. Use this diagram as a guide when arranging your classroom to make transitioning to whole-group and small-group activities easy for your young learners!

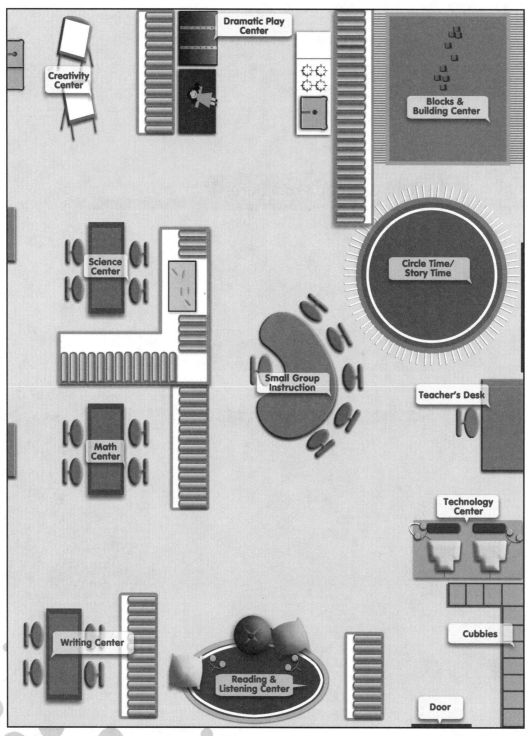

Planning My Classroom Layout

Use the space below to sketch your classroom layout. Consider areas for:

- ❏ Teacher's desk
- ❏ Children's cubbies
- ❏ Circle Time/Story Time
- ❏ Small Group Instruction

- ❏ Reading & Listening Center
- ❏ Writing Center
- ❏ Math Center
- ❏ Science Center

- ❏ Creativity Center
- ❏ Dramatic Play Center
- ❏ Blocks & Building Center
- ❏ Technology Center

Preparing Your Classroom

Scheduling Your Day

Establishing a consistent daily schedule helps both you and your children learn the daily routine, anticipate activities, and develop important skills.

What Makes a Big Day?

Each daily plan includes:

- Three whole-group Big Experiences
- A Small Group Instruction lesson
- Options for Small Group Intervention and One-to-One Follow-Up
- Theme-specific Learning Center activities

Look at the sample half-day and full-day schedules below. Then consider in your classroom. How much time would you spend on each activity in your Big Day?

Activity	Half-Day	Full-Day	My Big Day
Meet & Greet	10 minutes	10 minutes	
Big Experience 1 (Circle Time/Story Time)	20 minutes	25 minutes	
Learning Centers With Small Group Instruction	60 minutes	60 minutes	
Snack Time	10 minutes	10 minutes	
Big Experience 2 (Circle Time/Story Time)	20 minutes	25 minutes	
Outdoor Time	30 minutes	25 minutes	
Lunch		30 minutes	
Read Aloud: Children's Choice		15 minutes	
Quiet Time		60 minutes	
Songs and Fingerplays		10 minutes	
Big Experience 3 (Circle/Story Time)	20 minutes	25 minutes	
Learning Centers With Responsive Instruction		30 minutes	
Outdoor Time		25 minutes	
Closing	10 minutes	10 minutes	

Customizing Your Daily Schedule

Reflect on the number of minutes you want to spend on each activity, then use the chart below to create a daily schedule that meets your needs. List the time of day in the first column (e.g., 8:00 a.m.) and the day's activity in the second column (e.g., Morning Meeting). As you customize your daily plan, consider the following:

- Alternate sitting and listening activities (e.g., Circle Time or Story Time) with more active experiences (e.g., outdoor play or Learning Centers).
- Allow large blocks of time for purposeful play in Learning Centers.
- Expect the unexpected and allow for some flexibility in your day.

Our Cleanup Procedure

Time	Activity

Posting the Daily Schedule

Turn your daily schedule into an interactive display to help children learn the daily routine and develop skills such as sequencing events, making predictions, and understanding concepts of time order.

- List the day's activities along with a picture (e.g., a slide for outside time) on large, individual index cards or chart paper.
- Display the schedule at eye level within children's easy reach.
- Draw attention to the schedule as activities change. If you are using individual cards, have a child remove each card from the display as the activity is completed.
- Refer children to the schedule throughout the day to see what activity is next or anticipate upcoming activities.

Flexibility in Your Day

Though sticking to a daily schedule helps children feel secure, there will inevitably be times when you need to adjust your schedule for special occasions or events.

To help prepare children for schedule changes, consider the ideas in the chart below, then add some ideas of your own!

Special Occasion	Ideas to Try
Celebrations (e.g., birthdays, holidays, honoring achievements)	• Note the event in advance on a class calendar. • Create a display to count down the days until the big event. • Post a reminder to children and their families on Family Space (see page 71). • _____ _____
Field Trips (e.g., to the library, farmer's market, zoo, park)	• Use the field trip suggestions on the Engaging Families and Community pages of your *Teaching Guides* to plan ahead. • Send a letter home to notify families of the scheduled trip **at least two weeks** in advance. • Have a back-up date in case the trip is dependent on special criteria such as good weather conditions. • _____ _____
Classroom Visitors (e.g., parents, grandparents, members of the community)	• Refer to the suggestions in the Engaging Families and Community pages of your *Teaching Guides* and contact potential visitors before starting the theme. • Schedule the visit during a regular whole-group meeting time, such as Circle Time or Story Time. Contact the visitor a day before to confirm the time of the visit. • _____ _____

Establishing Daily Routines

Clear and consistent routines support classroom management and help children develop independence and self-control.

A Three-Step Approach

The time and effort you spend establishing routines at the start of the year will pay off later. Follow three easy steps to successfully establish routines in the first few weeks of school:

Step 1: Introduce the Routine Simplify the routine by breaking it up into manageable steps. Introduce each step one at a time, modeling what you expect children to do.

Step 2: Practice Provide multiple opportunities for children to practice the routine. Acknowledge and commend children for following the steps.

Step 3: Review and Revisit Monitor to make sure children understand the routine. Review and revisit routine steps whenever needed and return to **Step 1** and **Step 2**, if necessary.

Routines for Social-Emotional Development

Big Day for PreK includes routines to support children's social-emotional development. Use the Be Big in the Classroom poster to provide step-by-step guidance to help children:

- Listen to others
- Problem-solve
- Deal with emotions
- Try a new approach
- Share

Refer children to the poster throughout the year to help them develop self-awareness and self-regulation and hone the skills needed for positive interactions with their peers.

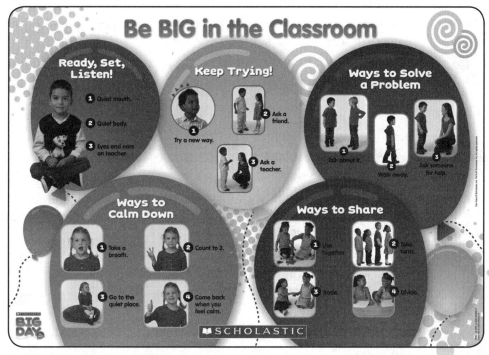

Be Big in the Classroom Poster

Routines in *Big Day for PreK*

Big Day for PreK includes classroom routines to start the day, end the day, and keep children engaged. Use the *Theme 1 Teaching Guide* to introduce routines gradually in the first few weeks. Then continue to use them regularly throughout the year!

Routine	Description	When to Use It
Meet and Greet Routines		
Arrive at School	*Step-by-step procedure for structuring the time between arrival and the start of the school day*	Daily
Today's Plan	*Sequence of daily activities to help children anticipate and understand what will happen throughout the day*	Daily
Who's Here Today?	*Sign-in routine which also helps you take attendance*	Daily
Classroom Helpers	*Procedure to keep track of classroom jobs and responsibilities*	Weekly
Morning Message	*Written message that includes predictable greeting and date; incorporates the Question of the Day and Daily News*	Daily
Daily News	*During Morning Message, children share one thing that happened to them*	2–3 times/ week
Question of the Day	*Question posed by teacher at the end of the Morning Message*	2–3 times/ week
Wrap-Up Routines		
Today's Report	*Written record of significant events of the school day*	Daily
How Did We Work Together?	*Children share something about how they worked well with others at school as part of Today's Report*	Daily
Sneak Preview	*An extension of Today's Report used to build excitement and anticipation for the next day*	Daily
Going Home	*Step-by-step procedures for structuring the time as children prepare to go home*	Daily
Engagement Routines		
Think, Turn, and Talk	*A quick way to get a large group of children to think and respond to a question*	As needed
Thumbs Up/ Thumbs Down	*A quick, visual way to engage all children in responding to a question nonverbally*	As needed
Make a Choice	*A kinesthetic way to involve children in responding nonverbally*	As needed

Managing Learning Centers

Establishing clear procedures and creating a system to help children choose Learning Centers effectively promote independence, while allowing you valuable time to work with small groups or one-to-one.

The Benefits of Learning Centers

Learning Center time is part of every Big Day! Not only do Learning Centers help children deepen and extend theme learning, but they also promote:

- Independence
- Self-discovery
- Decision-making skills
- Peer interaction and collaboration

With a little planning and preparation, well-managed Learning Centers can be a valuable part of a young child's instructional day—and a valuable opportunity for you to spend time providing targeted instruction to small groups and individuals.

Learning Centers in *Big Day for PreK*

Big Day for PreK supports you in implementing Learning Centers effectively throughout the year. The *Theme 1 Teaching Guide* provides explicit guidance to help you gradually introduce Learning Centers to young learners at the start of the year. When introducing Centers, remember to:

- Model and explain the activities children can do in each Center.
- Model how to choose a Center.
- Show children how to find and put away materials.
- Practice transitioning to different Centers.
- Teach the steps children take when they need help, have a question, or encounter a conflict.

Once children are comfortable choosing and navigating Learning Centers, turn to the Learning Centers tab of your *Teaching Guides* for ideas to help you tailor activities to deepen understanding of the topic of the theme week.

Learning Centers in Action

In *Big Day for PreK,* Learning Centers take place for one hour in the morning and, for full-day schedules, another hour in the afternoon. During this time, children might rotate between three or four Learning Centers, spending 15–20 minutes at each Center.

Once children are able to independently navigate Centers with ease, then you can simultaneously teach Small Group Instruction or Intervention or provide One-to-One Follow-Up. Take a look at the chart below for an example of 20-minute rotations in one classroom.

	Rotation 1	Rotation 2	Rotation 3
Learning Centers	Cyrus Adrienne Monique Von Christina Jelani Brett Janice	Alex Cris Dontaira Chad Cyrus Adrienne Monique Von	Christina Jelani Brett Janice Alex Cris Dontaira Chad
Small Group	Alex Cris Dontaira Chad	Christina Jelani Brett Janice	Cyrus Adrienne Monique Von

Making the Transition

Introduce and use a consistent signal to indicate when children rotate to a new activity. Signals might include:

- Clapping hands
- Blowing a whistle
- Dimming lights
- Singing or playing a "rotation" song
- Ringing a bell
- Raising a hand quietly

Whichever signal you choose, introduce it early on and practice, practice, practice! The time you spend up front introducing and practicing rotation procedures will help you with time-management in the long term.

Big Hint

Make transitions fun and educational! When learning about Things That Move in Theme 3, have children "drive" an imaginary car, bus, or plane to the next activity.

Helping Children Choose Centers

Create a system to help children independently choose Learning Centers. Reflect on the suggestions below, then choose a system that meets your children's needs.

Clothespin Choice

Attach a photo of each child's face to a clothespin. Make a sign for each Learning Center that accommodates clothespins for the maximum number of children who may be in the Center at one time. When children go to a Center, they clip their clothespin on a blank space. When spaces fill up, children know that the Center is full.

Center Passports

Create Center Passports with covers of different-colored construction paper and photos of each child. At each Learning Center, use pockets to indicate the maximum number of children who can be in the Center at a given time. Children place their Center Passports in a pocket. If all pockets are full, then they know they need to choose a different Center. Before transitioning to the next Center, children can "stamp" their Passports to show which Centers they visited that day.

Big Hint
Consider a management system (e.g., Center Passports) that will also help you track and record which Learning Centers children visit each day.

Center Necklaces

Use yarn and laminated index cards with Center names to create necklaces. Hang a specific number of color-coded necklaces (e.g., red for Reading & Listening Center, green for Science Center) to clearly indicate the maximum number of children who can be in each Center at a given time. Children visiting a Learning Center wear a Center Necklace to indicate their choice. When there are no necklaces available, the Center has reached capacity and children would make a different choice.

My Center Management System

Briefly describe **your** approach to helping children choose Learning Centers.

_____

_____

_____

_____

_____

_____

Managing Small Groups

Once clear procedures are in place for children to move from Center to Center independently, you can focus on providing targeted instruction to small groups.

Forming Small Groups

Big Day for PreK includes daily Small Group Instruction as well as optional Small Group Intervention activities. The *Theme 1 Teaching Guide* provides suggestions for setting up small groups at the start of the year. Refer to the tips below for year-round best practices.

- Keep groups small with no more than 5 children.
- Form heterogeneous groups for Small Group Instruction.
- Group children with similar learning needs when providing targeted skills instruction during Small Group Intervention.
- Regroup children as frequently as every week to build community and promote collaboration.
- Provide children with the option of working on an activity with a self-selected partner or independently, when applicable.

Announcing Small Group Assignments

The whole-group Meet and Greet time is a great opportunity for introducing small-group assignments. When reviewing the day's schedule using the Today's Plan routine (see *Professional Handbook* page 25), take a moment to also introduce small-group assignments. Consider the following tips to help children know and remember their small-group assignments:

Create a Visual Display This could be as simple as writing children's names on different-colored paper and posting the display on the wall. Help children find their name either by identifying the first letter or looking for their photograph. When it is time to meet for Small Group Instruction, hold up the group color that you will meet with first.

Make Group Necklaces Use yarn and card stock cut into shapes (e.g., triangle, square, circle). Write each child's name on a card stock shape, then string the yarn through to create a wearable reminder of children's group assignments. When it's Small Group Instruction time, hold up a shape cutout and, while outlining the shape, say, *I am meeting with the triangle group! Remember a triangle has three sides.*

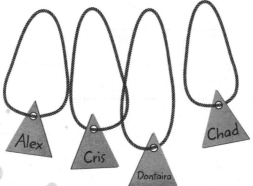

Making Small Group Rotations Easy!

A little preparation can go a long way to facilitate the transition to small groups. Consider the following suggestions to help you maximize instructional time and make small-group rotations run smoothly:

Green Means Go!

Consider using colors, animals, or shapes when assigning children to groups. For example, divide children into Green, Red, Yellow, and Blue groups. Call for groups by color when you are ready for Small Group Instruction (e.g., *In two minutes, I want the Green group to meet me at the Small Groups table.*). Not only will this make it easier for children to remember their groups, but it will also reinforce learning!

On the Move!

Create a rotation chart to help children anticipate when they will join their group at the Small Group Instruction table. Make it theme-related to reinforce learning and keep it fun! For example, during Theme 3, create a transportation-themed rotation chart. Cut out a paper Car, Bus, Airplane, and Truck and write children's names on each to form groups. Place these in order of rotation along a butcher paper "road." After meeting with the Car group, show you are ready for the Bus group by placing the Car cutout at the end of the line.

Signal Ahead!

Give children a two-minute warning so they can prepare to join the Small Group Instruction table. After two minutes, use a signal, such as a bell or whistle, to provide warning. Then signal again two minutes later to indicate that it is rotation time! Whatever signal you choose, be consistent and take time to have children practice, practice, practice!

Transitioning Throughout the Day

Transitioning to different activities throughout the day can be easy with a little preparation!

Signaling Transitions

Help children know when to transition from whole-group, to small-group, to independent activities with clear and consistent signals, such as:

- Ringing a bell
- Clapping your hands
- Singing or playing a special song
- Dimming lights
- Raising your hand
- Doing a countdown chant (e.g., *3-2-1, Learning Center time is done! 1-2-3, all eyes on me!*)

Provide a warning signal a few minutes before transition time to give children enough time to finish their activities and begin the cleanup procedure. Then use the preferred transition signal to indicate that it is time to move!

Transition Time Activities

Keep transition time engaging! Use different hand clap patterns or play "Simon Says" to make transitions interactive and educational. For theme-specific activities to try, look for the icon within each Big Experience in your *Teaching Guides* to help children sing, chant, or wiggle their way to the next activity. Not only will children have fun, but they will also deepen their understanding of key skills and concepts.

Big Hint
Try singing or whispering during transition time activities to help children stay focused!

Practice, Practice, Practice!

Transitioning can be challenging for some children. Spend time at the beginning of the year repeatedly practicing transitions so children know how to move quickly and quietly. Use a timer to time children as they practice to make a game out of transitioning quickly!

Remember to continue to practice small-group rotations throughout the year, whenever you reassign groups. This will not only help children know when to transition, but it will also help them remember their group assignments.

Using the Technology

Teaching and Learning Online

Big Day for PreK *includes innovative Web-based technology to support teachers, extend children's learning, and help families stay connected year-round.*

Why Is Technology Important?

Technology is fast becoming an integral part of our everyday lives. With instant messaging, chat, email, and social networking websites, Web-based technologies have long been bringing people together. But technology is not just about making communication easier; it's also about making information readily available and accessible to all. More and more we turn to the Internet to quickly access information at our fingertips.

Consider the importance of technology in your own life. Reflect on the list below and check all that apply.

*In the **last two weeks,** I have . . .*

- ❏ Sent/received an email.
- ❏ Sent/received a text message.
- ❏ Used an Internet search engine.
- ❏ Uploaded a video, image, or document.
- ❏ Downloaded a video, image, or document.
- ❏ Played a computer or video game.
- ❏ Logged into a social networking site.
- ❏ Read an online news or magazine article.
- ❏ Updated computer software.

- ❏ Made an online purchase.
- ❏ Read an online product review.
- ❏ Paid a bill online.
- ❏ Used an Internet travel site.
- ❏ Checked the weather online.
- ❏ Used an online dictionary/thesaurus.
- ❏ Other _____

 _____

 _____

Technology and the PreK Classroom

From high-tech toys to video games, child-friendly computers to MP3 players—our tech-savvy youngsters are what some call "digital natives" (Prensky, 2005). Preparing children for the future also means integrating the technology of today. *Big Day for PreK* uses technology as a tool to support teaching, enhance learning, and prepare children for life in the 21st century. Including technology in the PreK classroom means children:

- Learn important life skills.
- Benefit from additional audiovisual support.
- Can practice new skills in a "safe," nonjudgmental environment.

- _____

- _____

Introducing the Technology

Big Day for PreK recognizes the important role technology plays in the 21st century. To prepare children for kindergarten and beyond means making technology part of every "big day." With Teacher Space and Family Space, teachers, children, and families can access resources and information anytime, anywhere.

Teacher Space

Teacher Space (**http://bigday.scholastic.com**) is the online home for classroom resources, assessment, lesson planning, and managing family communication. Log on from any computer with an Internet connection to:

- Plan and customize your lessons.
- View teaching resources (e.g., *Teaching Guides, Professional Handbook, Songs and Fingerplays*) digitally!
- Download and print informal and formal assessment tools and teaching resources.
- Generate reports to monitor children's growth.
- Manage family communication on Family Space.

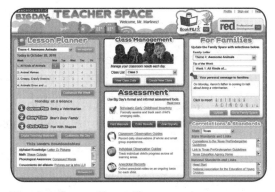

Teacher Space Home Page

BookFlix

With one-click access from Teacher Space and Family Space, this engaging online literacy resource can inspire a love of reading in children at school, at home, or from any computer with Internet access! BookFlix includes:

- Theme-related video storybooks.
- Nonfiction eBooks with optional language support.
- Fun, interactive literacy-building activities tailored to young learners.

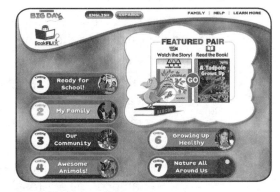

BookFlix Home Page

Family Space

Family Space (**http://bigdayfamily.scholastic.com**) is a bilingual communication tool that offers families a virtual window into their child's learning and enables all families to extend learning at home. Families can log in to Family Space to:

- Discover what children are learning that week.
- Read teacher messages and weekly tips.
- Download books to read together.
- Access educational activities and resources.

Family Space Home Page

Planning and Assessing With Teacher Space

Teacher Space is your online classroom planning and management tool.

Teacher Space Home Page

From the Teacher Space Home Page you can access:

Customized Lesson Planners Adjust activities and edit learning objectives to customize your day and week.

Downloadable Resources Print downloadable resources for the day's activities, letters to communicate with families, and certificates to recognize children's achievements.

Assessment and Reporting Record observations, print Scholastic Early Childhood Inventory (SECI) materials, enter results, and run reports at the class and child levels.

For Families Maintain the home-school connection by posting messages and tips on Family Space.

Quick Links Access BookFlix and the online professional development course with just one click.

Getting Started

When logging in to Teacher Space for the first time, you will need to create a teacher profile from a school or district computer.

1 Go to **http://bigday.scholastic.com** and enter the username and password provided to you by your district/school administrator.

2 From the **Create Teacher Profile** screen, enter the required information (e.g., your first and last name, email address) and create a new username and password.

Teacher Space Sign-In

My Username: _____   My Password: _____

3 Click the box next to **Display My Contact Information** if you would like your email address to appear on Family Space. Then click **Next**.

4 Enter required information for your class (e.g., Class Name, Class Username, Class Password, Session Dates). Share the class username and password with children and their families so they can log in to Family Space and BookFlix.

Class Username: _____   Class Password: _____

5 Click **Done** to save the information. Once your profile is complete, use your username and password to log in to Teacher Space from any computer with an Internet connection.

Create a Class

Use the Class Creation Wizard to add more classes and set up rosters.

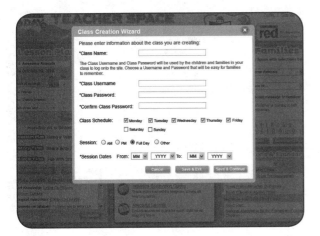

Directions

1 Log in to Teacher Space. From the Teacher Space Home Page, click **Create New Class** under **Class Management** to open the Class Creation Wizard.

2 Enter the required information (e.g., Class Name, Class Username, Class Password, Session Dates).

Technology Tip

Be sure to create a **Class Username** and **Class Password** that children and families will easily remember (e.g., the school name) as they will use this to log in to Family Space and BookFlix.

3 Once complete, click **Done** to save the class profile and go on to the Student Creation Wizard, or click **Cancel** to exit the Class Creation Wizard without saving the information.

Add a Student

Use the Student Creation Wizard to store information for each child.

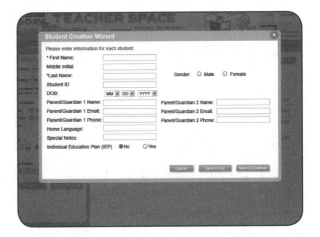

Directions

1 From the Teacher Space Home Page, choose a class from the **Class** pull-down menu under **Class Management**. Then click **View Class Data**.

2 Click **Add a Student** in the **Class Management** screen to open the Student Creation Wizard.

3 Enter the child's information in the Student Creation Wizard (e.g., First Name, Last Name, DOB, and any parent/guardian contact information).

4 Once complete, click **Save & Continue** to save the current profile and go on to create another, or click **Save & Exit** to save the profile and exit the Student Creation Wizard. Click **Cancel** to exit the Student Creation Wizard without saving.

Technology Tip

Click **Print Class Roster** on the **Class Management** screen to open a print preview window of the current class roster. Then click **Print** to print a roster that includes children's first and last names, gender, and IEPs.

Plan a Week

View weekly activities and objectives, add notes, and print the plan for the week.

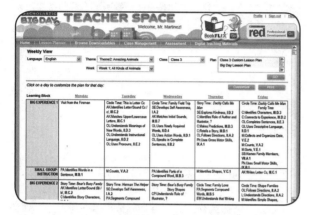

Directions

1. From the Teacher Space Home Page, choose a **theme** from the pull-down menu in the **Lesson Planner**.

2. Click a **week** in the calendar, then click the **Customize the Week** button to open the **Weekly View** screen for an overview of the week's activities and related learning objectives.

3. Scroll down to the **Reflections/Notes** box at the bottom of the **Weekly View** screen to type any lesson notes. Click **Save** to save weekly notes or **Cancel** to reset the **Reflections/Notes** box.

Technology Tip

The **Daily Notes** section of the **Weekly View** screen displays any notes added to a daily lesson to the **Reflections/Notes**, organized by day.

4. Click the **Print** button at the top of the **Weekly View** screen to open a print preview window. Click the **Print** button at the top to print the week's activities, objectives, and added notes.

Customize Your Lessons

Customize the activities and objectives in your lesson plans to meet your needs.

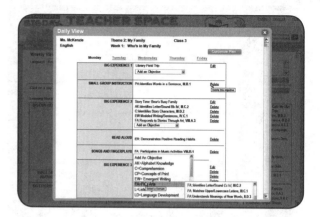

Directions

1. From the Teacher Space Home Page, choose a **theme** from the pull-down menu in the **Lesson Planner**.

2. Click a **week** in the calendar, then click **Customize the Week** to open the **Weekly View** screen.

3. Click **Customize Plan**. Type a name for your customized plan in the space provided, then click **Save**. The name will appear in the **Weekly View** screen.

4. Click a **day** link at the top of the calendar to open the **Daily View** window.

5. Click the **Edit** link to the right of an activity to make changes. Then click **Done**. Click the **Delete** link to remove an objective or select an objective from the **Add an objective** pull-down menu to add one.

6. Click **Save** to save your changes, **Cancel** to close the **Daily View** window and return to the **Weekly View** screen without saving, or **Print** to print the customized daily lesson plan.

Find and Print Resources

Access resources to teach lessons, assess learning, communicate with families, and recognize achievements.

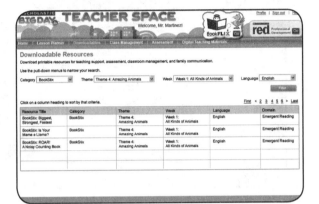

Directions

1 From the Teacher Space Home Page, click **Browse All** in the **Lesson Planner** to view the **Downloadable Resources** screen.

2 By default you will see all Downloadable Resources listed alphabetically by Resource Title. Use the pull-down menus at the top to filter resources by **Category**, **Theme**, and/or **Week**. Then click **Go**.

Technology Tip

You can access the resources you need for the week directly from the Teacher Space Home Page by clicking the links under **This Week's Downloadables** in the **Lesson Planner**.

3 Click the column heads to sort the list by **Resource Title**, **Category**, **Theme**, **Week**, **Language**, or **Domain**. Click a **Resource Title** link from the list to download the resource.

4 Open the downloaded resource in Adobe Acrobat. Click **File** in the Adobe Acrobat toolbar. Then select **Print** from the pull-down menu to print the resource.

Print Pathways to Readiness Continuums

Download and print the continuums to monitor developmental progress.

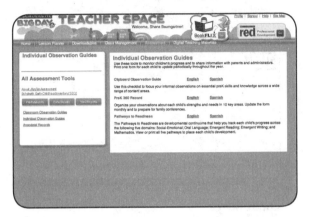

Directions

1 From the Teacher Space Home Page, click the **Individual Observation Guides** link in the **Assessment** section to view the **Individual Observation Guides** screen.

2 Click the **English** link to the right of **Pathways to Readiness** to download the continuums in English or the **Spanish** link to download them in Spanish.

Technology Tip

Find the Individual Observation Guides, including the Pathways to Readiness continuums, by clicking **Browse All** from the Teacher Space Home Page to view the **Downloadable Resources** screen. Select **Individual Observation** from the **Category** pull-down menu, then click **Go**.

3 Open the downloaded resource in Adobe Acrobat. Click **File** in the Adobe Acrobat toolbar. Then select **Print** from the pull-down menu to print the resource.

Print Observation Guides

Download and print informal assessment tools to record classroom observations.

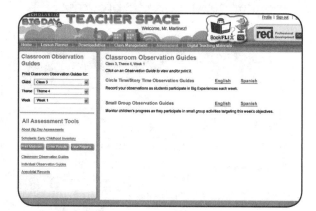

Print Records and Checklists

Print the Clipboard Observation and PreK 360 Record to monitor progress.

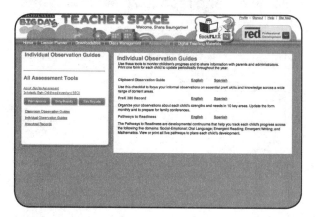

Directions

1. From the Teacher Space Home Page, click **Classroom Observation Guides** in the **Assessment** section to view the **Classroom Observation Guides** screen.

> **Technology Tip**
>
> Find Circle Time/Story Time and Small Group Observation Guides by clicking **Browse All** from the Teacher Space Home Page to open the **Downloadable Resources** screen. Select **Classroom Observation** from the **Category** pull-down menu, then select the theme and week and click **Go**.

2. Select the **class**, **theme**, and **week** from the pull-down menus in the left navigation bar. Then click **Submit**.

3. Click the **English** or **Spanish** link to the right of **Circle Time/Story Time Observation Guide** or **Small Group Observation Guide** to view the selected guide for the specified theme and week.

4. To print the **Circle Time/Story Time Observation Guide**, click **File** in the Adobe Acrobat toolbar. Then select **Print.** For the **Small Group Observation Guide**, click the **Print** button.

Directions

1. From the Teacher Space Home Page, click **Individual Observation Guides** in the **Assessment** section of the Teacher Space Home Page to view the **Individual Observation Guides** screen.

2. Click the **English** or **Spanish** link to the right of **Clipboard Observation Guide** or **PreK 360 Record** to download the selected resource.

3. Open the downloaded resource in Adobe Acrobat. Click **File** in the Adobe Acrobat toolbar. Then select **Print** from the pull-down menu to print the resource.

> **Technology Tip**
>
> To print multiple copies of the same resource, select **Print** from the pull-down menu, then adjust the number of **Copies** before clicking **Print**.

Enter Anecdotal Records

Enter anecdotes online to record observations for individual children.

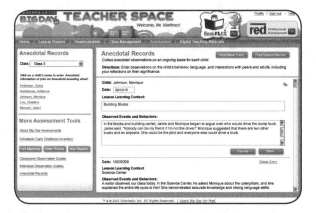

Directions

1 From the Teacher Space Home Page, click **Anecdotal Records** in the **Assessment** section to view the **Anecdotal Records** screen.

2 Select a **class** from the pull-down menu in the left navigation bar. Then click a **child's name** from the roster to view that child's **Anecdotal Record** screen.

3 To enter anecdotes online, click **Date,** then click a **day** on the calendar to select a date for the observation.

4 Click the box under **Lesson/Learning Context** to type the event place and time. Click the box under **Observed Event and Behaviors** to type a description.

Technology Tip

Download a blank Anecdotal Record form by clicking **Print Blank Form** from a child's **Anecdotal Records** screen. Then select **Print** from the **File** pull-down menu in the Adobe Acrobat toolbar.

5 Click **Save** to save and automatically generate a new blank online entry. Click **Cancel** to clear the entry without saving. Click **Print Student Record** to print all saved entries for that child.

Print SECI Materials

Print instructions and materials for the Scholastic Early Childhood Inventory.

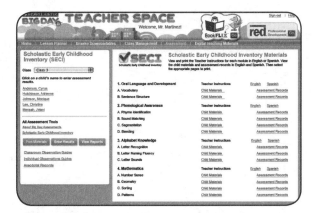

Directions

1 From the Teacher Space Home Page, click **Print Materials** in the **Assessment** section to view the **Scholastic Early Childhood Inventory Materials** screen.

2 Click the **English** or **Spanish** link to the right of a module to download the Teacher Instructions for that module.

3 Click the **Child Materials** link to the right of a subtest to download Child Materials for that subtest in English and Spanish. Click the **Assessment Records** link to download the Assessment Records for that subtest in English and Spanish.

4 Open the downloaded resource in Adobe Acrobat. Click **File** in the Adobe Acrobat toolbar. Then select **Print** from the pull-down menu to print the resource.

Technology Tip

To print Teacher Instructions for a specific subtest or to print Child Materials or Assessment Records in a specific language, open the resource in Adobe Acrobat. Select **Print** from the Adobe Acrobat **File** menu. Click **Pages,** then type the desired page range before clicking **Print**.

Enter SECI Results

Record children's scores online to run reports and track growth.

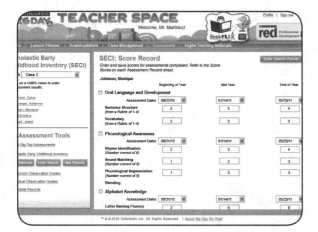

Generate and Print Reports

Run SECI reports to monitor and share children's developmental progress.

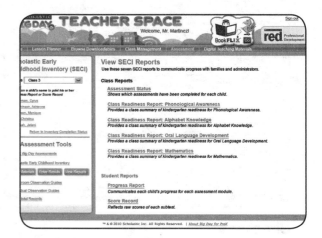

Directions

1 From the Teacher Space Home Page, click **Enter Results** in the **Assessment** section to view the **SECI: Score Record** screen.

2 Select a **class** from the pull-down menu in the left navigation bar, then click a **child's name** to open the **SECI: Score Record** screen for that child.

Technology Tip

Click **Enter Spanish Results** in the upper right corner of the **SECI: Score Record** screen to enter results for the Spanish administration of the SECI.

3 Click **Select Date,** then click a **day** on the calendar to select the date of assessment.

4 Click the **boxes** to the right of each subtest and type the child's scores.

5 Click **Save** to save scores or **Cancel** to clear changes without saving.

Directions

1 From the Teacher Space Home Page, click **View Reports** in the **Assessment** section to view the **SECI Reports** screen.

2 Select a **class** from the pull-down menu in the left navigation bar.

3 To view a class-level report, click a **report name** under **Class Reports**. To view a child-level report, first click a **child's name** in the Class List in the left navigation bar. Then click either **Progress Report** or **Score Report** to view the child's report in a pop-up window.

4 Click **Print** to print the report to share with families or administrators.

Post Messages to Families

Display a message on Family Space to update families on classroom learning and events.

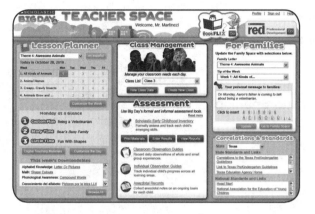

Directions

1 From the Teacher Space Home Page, click the **message box** in the **For Families** section.

2 Type your message in the space provided, then click the **Update** button to save the message and display it on **Family Space**.

> ### Technology Tip
>
> If writing a message in Spanish, click a **Spanish character** to insert it into the message box as needed.

3 Click the **Go to Family Space** button to see the message live on the Family Space Home Page.

Display a Tip and Theme Letter on Family Space

Keep families informed of children's learning and share at-home tips.

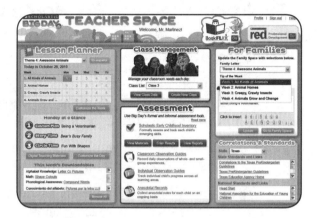

Directions

1 From the Teacher Space Home Page, select the **theme** and **week** from the pull-down menus in the **For Families** section.

2 Click the **Update** button to automatically display the Theme Letter and Tip of the Week on **Family Space**.

> ### Technology Tip
>
> Download and print **Theme Letters** to send home. From the **Downloadable Resources** screen, select **Family Letter** from the **Category** pull-down menu and the current theme from the **Theme** pull-down menu. Then click **Go.** Families can also view the letters online by clicking the **View Family Letter** link in the **What We Are Learning** section of Family Space.

3 Click the **Go to Family Space** button to view the letter and tip live on the Family Space Home Page.

Building Literacy With BookFlix

BookFlix builds a love of reading and learning with online access to animated children's books and literacy games.

Exploring the BookFlix Home Page

Take a moment to get familiar with the BookFlix Home Page. Mark up the image using the directions below.

1. Children and families can view BookFlix in English or Spanish. Locate and **circle** the **English and Spanish buttons** that appear on the Home Page.

2. **Star** the area you would click to view the Reading Pairs for **Theme 3, Our Community**.

3. X marks the spot! Place an **X** where you would click to **Browse All** online reading titles.

4. **Underline** the **link to literacy-building tips for families** to support children's online literacy experience at home.

Big Hint
When hosting Family Night, project BookFlix onto an interactive whiteboard. Then support family members as they use the whiteboard to navigate BookFlix.

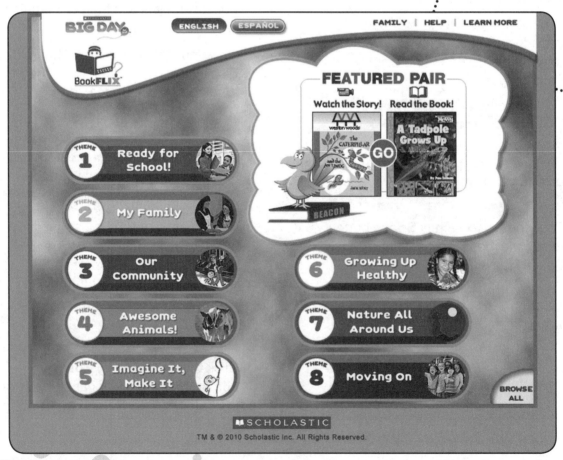

BookFlix Home Page

BookFlix Seek & Find

Explore the online video storybooks, content-area eBooks, and exciting resources and features on BookFlix. Use the username and password you created for Teacher Space to log in to BookFlix (**http://bigdaybookflix.scholastic.com**) or simply click **Go** in the BookFlix icon while logged in to Teacher Space (**http://bigday.scholastic.com**). Seek and find the information to complete the tasks below.

Information to Seek	My Findings
Find the **two nonfiction-fiction Reading Pairs** for Theme 3, Our Community.	What are the **titles** of the Theme 3 online readings?
Watch a **video storybook**.	*One thing I liked about the video storybook is . . .*
Read the **nonfiction eBook** paired with that video storybook.	What happens when you place your cursor on a **yellow highlighted word**? What happens when you click the **ear icon?**
Play one or more **Puzzlers!**—interactive educational games related to the selected Reading Pair.	Which of the **Puzzlers!** did you choose? Describe the activity.
Learn more about the fictional story **author**.	*One interesting thing I learned is . . .*
Explore an age-appropriate **Web link** related to the selected Reading Pair.	How was the Web link: _____ related to the online readings?

Learning Online With BookFlix

With easy online access to the video storybooks, nonfiction eBooks, and interactive literacy games, BookFlix is ideal for use in *all* learning environments! Consider the suggested uses below and add some ideas of your own!

Learning Environment	Ideas
Big Experiences	• Project BookFlix onto a screen or interactive whiteboard to show children how to use the website. • Project BookFlix onto a screen or interactive whiteboard to bring read alouds to life. • _____
Small Group Instruction	• Guide a small group to practice literacy skills with Puzzlers! activities. • _____
Learning Centers	• Have children practice computer skills while visiting BookFlix in the Technology Center. • Encourage children to extend theme learning through interactive reading experiences. • _____
With Families	• Get the word out! Demonstrate how to use BookFlix during family orientation or open house. • Provide families with a list of places in the community where they can access computers with an Internet connection (e.g., public library). • _____

Engaging Families With Family Space

Families can log in to Family Space to stay informed and support their children's learning and progress toward kindergarten readiness.

Introducing Families to Family Space

Family Space is a place just for families. Parents and caregivers can log in to Family Space (**http://bigdayfamily.scholastic.com**) from any computer with an Internet connection to:

- Keep informed about classroom learning.
- Read weekly tips for extending learning beyond the classroom.
- Visit BookFlix to build literacy at home.
- Anticipate developmental milestones with the Kindergarten Readiness Indicators.
- Download books and educational resources.

So how can families get started? Begin by getting the word out! Go to Teacher Space (**http://bigday.scholastic.com**) and download the About Family Space family letter in English or Spanish. Distribute the letter to families to provide them all the information they need to access the exciting online games, activities, and resources.

Support families by highlighting key features of the website during open house or orientation. Look at the Family Space Home Page below. Place a star next to three key features you would want to highlight.

Big Hint

Consider hosting evening workshops for families. Share tips and best practices for using online resources and conducting dialogic readings at home.

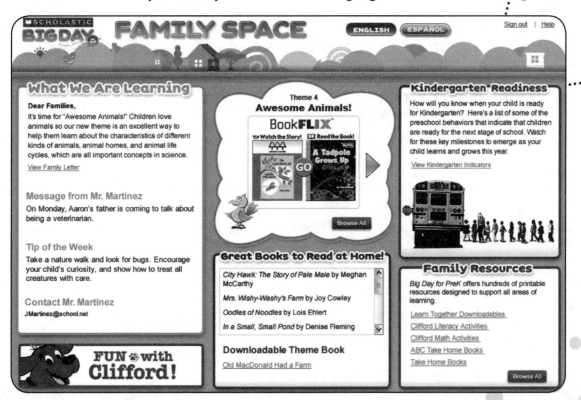

Family Space Home Page

Exploring Resources on Family Space

Encourage families to visit Family Space often to build and strengthen the home-school connection year-round. Complete the tasks below, then use the prompts to guide your reflection.

Tasks	Reflection
1 Read the family Theme Letter and Tip of the Week included under **What We Are Learning.**	*One way the Tip of the Week supports theme learning is:*
2 Click **Fun With Clifford**, then click to begin an interactive online story.	*One thing I like about Fun With Clifford online activities is:*
3 Scroll the book titles under **Great Books to Read at Home!** Then click the link to view the **Downloadable Theme Book.**	*One way I plan to encourage families to read with their children at home is:*
4 Click to view two downloadable resource links under **Family Resources.**	*The resources I explored were* _____ *and* _____ . *One way I can support families to use these resources is:*

Assessing Young Learners

Watching Children Learn and Grow

Young learners grow in leaps and bounds! Big Day for PreK *includes tools and resources to help you assess and monitor growth and development, share your observations with families, and plan responsive instruction.*

Big Principles of *Big Day for PreK* Assessments

Big Day for PreK includes a comprehensive, multifaceted approach to monitoring growth and learning with informal assessment tools, including downloadable classroom observation guides, individual observation guides and whole-child snapshots, anecdotal records, and portfolio assessment, as well as the formal assessment tool, Scholastic Early Childhood Inventory (SECI).

Big Day for PreK assessments were developed based on the following key principles to ensure they:

- Benefit children.
- Include a variety of formal and informal tools and methods.
- Recognize that reliability and validity increase with children's age.
- Are age-appropriate in both content and approach.
- Use age-appropriate language.
- Bring teachers and families together to support children's development and learning progress.

Pathways to Readiness

Big Day for PreK includes developmental continuums to help you monitor children's progress along the path to kindergarten readiness. These Pathways to Readiness continuums provide age-appropriate research-based benchmarks to help you monitor children's developmental progress in five key domains:

- Social-Emotional Development
- Oral Language Development
- Emergent Reading
- Emergent Writing
- Mathematics Development

The formal and informal assessment tools in *Big Day for PreK* provide you with information to help you update the Pathways to Readiness continuums regularly throughout the year and plan instructional support to get children kindergarten-ready.

Assessing Young Learners

Assessments, both formal and informal, give insight into children's strengths and needs so that you can plan instruction and communicate progress throughout the year.

Formal Assessment

Formal assessments are standardized measures administered regularly to monitor children's progress over time. The formal assessment in *Big Day for PreK* is the Scholastic Early Childhood Inventory, or SECI, and is available in English and Spanish. Administer the SECI three times a year to formally assess the skills shown to be most highly predictive of later academic success:

- Oral Language Development
- Phonological Awareness
- Alphabet Knowledge
- Mathematics

You can print SECI materials, enter scores, and run data-rich reports directly from Teacher Space **(http://bigday.scholastic.com).**

Informal Assessment

Informal assessments are daily, ongoing observations to help you recognize children's strengths, learning needs, and developmental milestones. You can download and print the following *Big Day for PreK* informal assessment tools (in English or Spanish) from Teacher Space:

- Circle Time/Story Time Observation Guides
- Small Group Observation Guides
- Clipboard Observation Guide
- PreK 360 Record
- Anecdotal Records

Reflect

What are two benefits of assessing young learners?

1. _____

2. _____

Monitoring Learning With Assessments

Use Big Day for PreK *formal and informal assessment tools to help you monitor children's development, adapt instruction to meet their developmental needs, and partner with families to guide children along the path to kindergarten readiness.*

	Assessment	Purpose	When to Assess
FORMAL	**Scholastic Early Childhood Inventory (SECI)**	Get a formal snapshot of each child's progress in skill areas that are most predictive of kindergarten readiness.	**Three times a year:** • Beginning-of-year, for baseline • Middle-of-year (after Theme 4), to measure progress • End-of-year, to measure proficiency
INFORMAL	**Classroom Observation Guides:** • Circle Time/ Story Time • Small Group	Observe children's progress toward meeting learning outcomes and plan One-to-One Follow-Up and Small Group Intervention.	**Daily,** based on data gathered during the Observe moments in Circle Time/Story Time and Small Group Instruction
	Individual Observation: PreK 360 Record	Summarize the strengths and needs of the whole child across skill domains.	**Two to three times a year** or as needed to prepare for parent conferences
	Individual Observation: Clipboard Observation	Track a child's understanding of key skills and concepts within specific domain areas.	**Once a theme (monthly)** or as each child acquires new skills
	Anecdotal Records	Record specific events that reflect each child's development over time.	**Daily,** as needed
	Show & Grow Portfolios	Collect authentic work samples throughout the year as a record of each child's progress.	**Continually,** to include work samples, anecdotal records, observation tools, and assessment results

Assessment Overview from *Big Day for PreK Professional Handbook*

What to Look For	Next Steps
Progress across four skill areas: • Oral Language • Phonological Awareness • Alphabet Knowledge • Mathematics	• Plan responsive instruction for children who demonstrate need for additional support. See *Teaching Guides* for intervention ideas. • Form small groups according to children's needs. • Consult with school personnel or specialists about children for whom you have serious concerns.
Development and progress in meeting learning outcomes in essential skill areas	• Refer to Responsive Instruction pages in the *Teaching Guide* for One-to-One Follow-Up and Small Group Intervention suggestions. • Form small groups according to children's strengths and needs.
Evidence of progress or milestones achieved in the 10 key domain areas	• Provide One-to-One Follow-Up or Small Group Intervention in key areas. • Share progress with families during conferences.
New skills demonstrated throughout the year	• Incorporate observations from the Clipboard as you update children's progress along the Pathways to Readiness continuums. • Share observations with families during conferences.
• Typical or atypical behaviors • Milestones	• Anticipate potential triggers for each child. • Note observed milestones on the Pathways to Readiness continuums. • Choose anecdotes to share with families or colleagues.
• Progress in development of skills • Range of interests across content areas	• Gather additional work samples in underrepresented areas. • Reflect on strengths and areas of need. • Choose work samples to share with families.

PATHWAYS TO READINESS

Using the Pathways to Readiness

Use the Pathways to Readiness continuums to monitor and communicate children's developmental progress toward kindergarten readiness throughout the year.

Tracking Individual Growth

The Pathways to Readiness continuums help you track each child's progress in five key domains: **Social-Emotional Development**, **Oral Language Development**, **Emergent Reading**, **Emergent Writing**, and **Mathematics Development**. You can find the Pathways to Readiness continuums on pages 74–83 of the *Professional Handbook* or download and print them directly from Teacher Space (see page 67).

Use information from the Scholastic Early Childhood Inventory (SECI), your own classroom observations, and input from families and caregivers to place children along the continuums in one of the following four stages of development:

- Pre-Emergent
- Beginning
- Emerging
- Developed

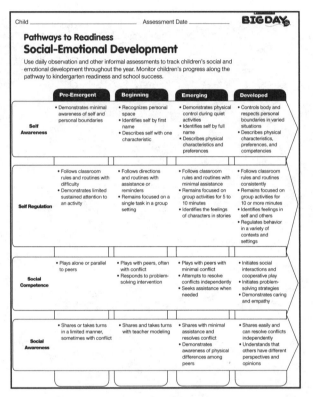

Pathways to Readiness: Social-Emotional Development

Monitoring Progress All Year Long

Continue to update and revisit the continuums throughout the year to monitor children's progress on the pathway to kindergarten readiness.

Start-of-Year At the start of the school year, use your initial SECI results and observations to establish a baseline for later comparison.

Mid-Year Update continuums each time you administer the SECI, before family conferences, at the end of a theme, or any time you observe a milestone. Meet with families to share results and learn more about each child.

End-of-Year Update continuums at the end-of-year and use the results to communicate accomplishments, strengths, and areas of need with children's families and future teachers.

What to Look For

Each child is unique and develops in his or her own way, and at his or her own pace. Use the Pathways to Readiness to look for overall progress, rather than expecting a child to be at a particular place on the continuum at the start or end of year.

The pathways benchmarks can help you recognize children's growth and alert you to areas that may require further attention. Use the chart below to plan support, celebrate achievements, and challenge young learners.

If . . .	Then . . .
A child progresses to Emergent or Developed categories	• Celebrate achievements. • Refer to Enrichment modifications suggested in the Responsive Instruction pages of the *Teaching Guides* to enhance daily Big Experiences. • Share progress with families, administrators, and the child's future teacher.
A child remains in Pre-Emergent or Beginning categories in many areas at mid-year	• Refer to Responsive Instruction pages of the *Teaching Guides* to provide One-to-One Follow-Up. • Conference with families to learn more about the child. Discuss ways to use the online resources available on Family Space and BookFlix. • Discuss your findings with a school specialist to determine if the child may need further assessment and/or intervention.
A child has regressed in one or more areas	• Compare results to information gathered through daily Observation Guides and Anecdotal Records. • Discuss your findings with a school specialist to determine if the child may need further assessment and/or intervention.
A child's progress in one skill or module is dramatically different from progress in other skills or modules.	• Ask families to share their own observations. • Discuss your findings with a school specialist to determine if the child may need further assessment and/or intervention.

Observing Children in Whole Group

Big Day for PreK *includes built-in daily opportunities for focused observations during each whole-class Big Experience.*

Focusing Your Class Observations

Look for the 📋 Observe icon when using your *Teaching Guides* to teach the three daily Big Experiences. The **Observe** features identify key skills and behaviors to focus your Circle Time/Story Time classroom observations.

Circle Time/Story Time Observation Guide

Every child is an individual with his or her own needs. The **Circle Time/Story Time Observation Guide** helps you monitor progress and identify children's learning needs. Download and print the **Circle Time/Story Time Observation Guide** for each week from Teacher Space, then record names of children who demonstrate the focus skill and those who need follow-up.

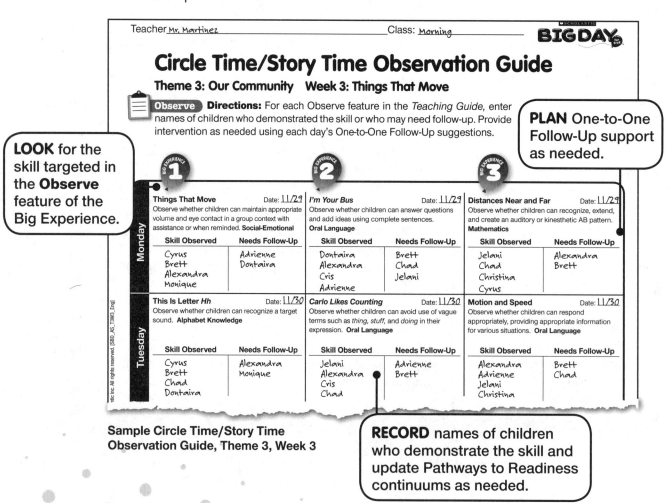

Sample Circle Time/Story Time
Observation Guide, Theme 3, Week 3

Planning Responsive Instruction

Children benefit from individual attention and focused one-to-one instruction. Use your Circle Time/Story Time Observation Guides to choose **One-to-One Follow-Up** suggestions from the chart on the **Responsive Instruction** pages of your *Teaching Guides*. Set aside some time during Learning Centers to spend a minute or two with each child who could benefit from One-to-One Follow-Up.

One-to-One Follow-Up

Use these suggestions to provide intervention for today's learning during Learning Center time or other times.

Observe	If ...	Then ...
1 Circle Time **This Is Letter *Hh*** Observe whether children can recognize a target sound. ALPHABET KNOWLEDGE	A child needs support recognizing the sound /h/ ...	Play a game of "Hot and Cold." • Say the word *hot*, emphasizing the sound /h/. Ask the child to repeat the word and echo the sound with you several times. • Tell the child that you are going to say several words. If a word starts with /h/, the child should say *hot*. If a word starts with another sound, the child should say *cold*. • Play the game until the child can recognize the initial /h/ sound in words.
2 Story Time ***Carlo Likes Counting*** Observe whether children can avoid use of vague terms such as *thing, stuff,* and *doing* in their expression. ORAL LANGUAGE	A child needs assistance to use specific vocabulary as they pick up classroom objects on their "bus rides" ...	Model the child's sentence with the specific vocabulary terms. **Teacher:** *What did you pick up on your bus ride?* **Child:** *I picked up some things.* **Teacher:** *When you say things, I'm not sure what you are talking about. I see that you picked up some blocks. Now you say it!* Continue cueing with the names of other objects the child picked up during the bus activity.
3 Circle Time **Motion and Speed** Observe whether children can respond appropriately, providing appropriate information for various situations. ORAL LANGUAGE	A child needs more support to provide information about objects and how they travel down the ramp ...	Practice sharing information. **Teacher:** *What did you roll down the ramp?* **Child:** *I like building ramps and things with blocks.* **Teacher:** *It is fun to build things, but we're talking about rolling things down the ramp. Jared rolled a ball down the ramp. Karin rolled a car down the ramp. What did you roll down the ramp?* **Child:** *I rolled a crayon down the ramp.* **Teacher:** *Now you are talking about the same thing we are talking about. That's great!*

Theme 3 Teaching Guide, **Week 3, Tuesday**

Reflect

Look at the Tuesday row in the sample Circle Time/Story Time Observation Guide (page 84). Which children might benefit from One-to-One Follow-Up?

_____

_____

What is one idea you have to support Brett with Oral Language Development?

_____

_____

_____

Observing Children in Small Groups

Daily Small Group Instruction provides an opportunity for meaningful teacher-child interactions, immediate teacher feedback, and close observation of targeted skills.

Focusing Your Small Group Observations

Small Group Instruction activities focus on building literacy (Monday, Wednesday, and Friday) and mathematics skills (Tuesday and Thursday). Each Small Group Instruction lesson in the Responsive Instruction pages of your *Teaching Guides* includes an 📋Observe. Use the **Observe** feature to evaluate how well children demonstrate a specific skill and identify those who might benefit from Small Group Intervention.

Small Group Observation Guide

Use the downloadable **Small Group Observation Guide** for each week to quickly note which children demonstrate the skill and which need additional support. Schedule additional Small Group Intervention for children who need follow-up support.

SCHOLASTIC BIG DAY Print

Teacher: Mr. Martinez   **Class:** Morning

Small Groups Observation Guide
Theme 3: Our Community Week 3: Things That Move

Directions: For each child, observe the skills demonstrated during daily Small Group Activities. Record whether each skills was observed, and note those who may need follow-up. Provide intervention as needed using each day's Small Groups Intervention suggestions. Include notes in each box to record further details about your observations.

Day	Monday	Tuesday	Wednesday	Thursday	Friday
Title	Segments Syllables **Phonological Awareness**	Mimic, Recognize, and Extend Kinesthetic and Auditory AB Patterns **Mathematics**	Delete a Syllable From a Word **Phonological Awareness**	Mimic, Recognize, and Extend Kinesthetic and Auditory AB Patterns **Mathematics**	Write the Letter Hh **Emergent Writing**
Observe whether children can...	identify syllables in words.	recognize, extend, and create an auditory or kinesthetic AB pattern.	segment syllables in words.	recognize, extend, and create an auditory or kinesthetic AB pattern.	control the pencil and approximate letter forms.
Name					
Cyrus Anderson	Date: 11/29 [✓] Skill Observed [ ] Needs Follow-Up	Date: 11/30 [✓] Skill Observed [ ] Needs Follow-Up	Date: 12/1 [✓] Skill Observed [ ] Needs Follow-Up	Date: 12/2 [✓] Skill Observed [ ] Needs Follow-Up	Date: 12/3 [ ] Skill Observed [✓] Needs Follow-Up Had difficulty with lowercase "h."
Adrienne Hutchinson	Date: 11/29 [✓] Skill Observed [ ] Needs Follow-Up	Date: 11/30 [ ] Skill Observed [ ] Needs Follow-Up Had trouble mimicking auditory AB patterns.	Date: 12/1 [✓] Skill Observed [ ] Needs Follow-Up	Date: 12/2 [ ] Skill Observed [✓] Needs Follow-Up Able to recognize AB pattern but unable to create one.	Date: 12/3 [✓] Skill Observed [ ] Needs Follow-Up
Monique Johnson	Date: 11/29 [✓] Skill Observed [ ] Needs Follow-Up	Date: 11/30 [ ] Skill Observed [✓] Needs Follow-Up Unable to create an AB pattern.	Date: 12/1 [✓] Skill Observed [ ] Needs Follow-Up	Date: 12/2 [✓] Skill Observed [ ] Needs Follow-Up	Date: 12/3 [✓] Skill Observed [ ] Needs Follow-Up

Sample Small Group Observation Guide, Theme 3, Week 3

USE intervention suggestions from the Responsive Instruction pages to plan follow-up support.

NOTE details to help you tailor follow-up intervention.

One way I might support Adrienne with patterns is:

_____

_____

_____

Planning Responsive Instruction

Use your daily observations to plan targeted support. Refer to the **Responsive Instruction** pages in your *Teaching Guides* for suggested Small Group Intervention activities.

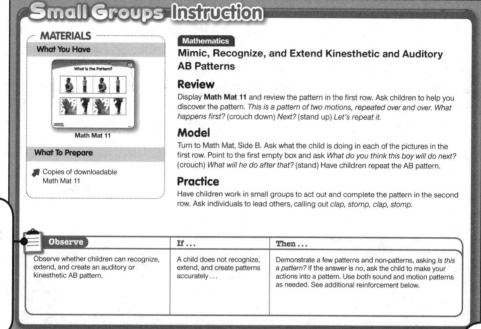

USE the Observe chart to provide children with immediate follow-up support.

PLAN additional targeted intervention for children who could use more support.

Theme 3 Teaching Guide, **Week 3, Tuesday**

Reflect

Look at the Tuesday column in the sample Small Group Observation Guide (page 86). How might you use the suggestions above to provide support to the children in Mr. Martinez's class?

_____

_____

_____

Using Checklists and Records

Big Day for PreK *includes informal assessment tools to help you assess the whole child, individualize instruction, and communicate with families year-round.*

Clipboard Observation Guide

Download and print a Clipboard Observation Guide **once per theme** (or monthly) to monitor each child's progress in nine key areas: Oral Language Development, Emergent Reading & Writing, Mathematics, Social-Emotional Development, Science and Health, Social Studies, Fine Arts, Physical Development, and Technology and Media. Take the guide with you and use the checklists to help you observe children during various activities throughout the day. Revisit the Clipboard Observation Guide when planning instruction or updating Pathways to Readiness continuums.

RECORD the date you observed the child demonstrate the skill.

One way this guide would help me individualize instruction is:

_____

_____

_____

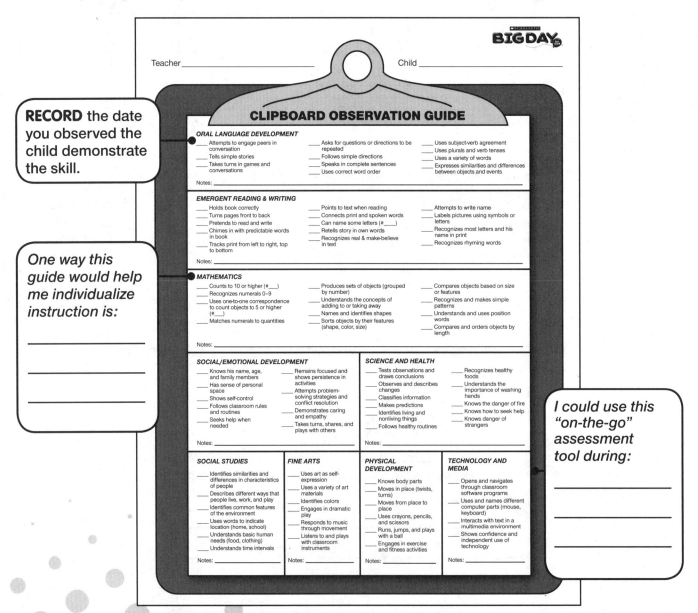

CLIPBOARD OBSERVATION GUIDE

Teacher _____   Child _____

ORAL LANGUAGE DEVELOPMENT
- Attempts to engage peers in conversation
- Tells simple stories
- Takes turns in games and conversations
- Asks for questions or directions to be repeated
- Follows simple directions
- Speaks in complete sentences
- Uses correct word order
- Uses subject-verb agreement
- Uses plurals and verb tenses
- Uses a variety of words
- Expresses similarities and differences between objects and events

Notes: _____

EMERGENT READING & WRITING
- Holds book correctly
- Turns pages front to back
- Pretends to read and write
- Chimes in with predictable words in book
- Tracks print from left to right, top to bottom
- Points to text when reading
- Connects print and spoken words
- Can name some letters (#___)
- Retells story in own words
- Recognizes real & make-believe in text
- Attempts to write name
- Labels pictures using symbols or letters
- Recognizes most letters and his name in print
- Recognizes rhyming words

Notes: _____

MATHEMATICS
- Counts to 10 or higher (#___)
- Recognizes numerals 0–9
- Uses one-to-one correspondence to count objects to 5 or higher (#___)
- Matches numerals to quantities
- Produces sets of objects (grouped by number)
- Understands the concepts of adding to or taking away
- Names and identifies shapes
- Sorts objects by their features (shape, color, size)
- Compares objects based on size or features
- Recognizes and makes simple patterns
- Understands and uses position words
- Compares and orders objects by length

Notes: _____

SOCIAL/EMOTIONAL DEVELOPMENT
- Knows his name, age, and family members
- Has sense of personal space
- Shows self-control
- Follows classroom rules and routines
- Seeks help when needed
- Remains focused and shows persistence in activities
- Attempts problem-solving strategies and conflict resolution
- Demonstrates caring and empathy
- Takes turns, shares, and plays with others

Notes: _____

SCIENCE AND HEALTH
- Tests observations and draws conclusions
- Observes and describes changes
- Classifies information
- Makes predictions
- Identifies living and nonliving things
- Follows healthy routines
- Recognizes healthy foods
- Understands the importance of washing hands
- Knows the danger of fire
- Knows how to seek help
- Knows danger of strangers

Notes: _____

SOCIAL STUDIES
- Identifies similarities and differences in characteristics of people
- Describes different ways that people live, work, and play
- Identifies common features of the environment
- Uses words to indicate location (home, school)
- Understands basic human needs (food, clothing)
- Understands time intervals

Notes: _____

FINE ARTS
- Uses art as self-expression
- Uses a variety of art materials
- Identifies colors
- Engages in dramatic play
- Responds to music through movement
- Listens to and plays with classroom instruments

Notes: _____

PHYSICAL DEVELOPMENT
- Knows body parts
- Moves in place (twists, turns)
- Moves from place to place
- Uses crayons, pencils, and scissors
- Runs, jumps, and plays with a ball
- Engages in exercise and fitness activities

Notes: _____

TECHNOLOGY AND MEDIA
- Opens and navigates through classroom software programs
- Uses and names different computer parts (mouse, keyboard)
- Interacts with text in a multimedia environment
- Shows confidence and independent use of technology

Notes: _____

I could use this "on-the-go" assessment tool during:

_____

_____

_____

Clipboard Observation Guide

PreK 360 Record

Use this tool to organize your ongoing observations and summarize children's progress within each domain. Download and print a PreK 360 Record for each child **two to three times a year** to prepare for and guide discussion during scheduled family conferences and give administrators and future teachers a comprehensive picture of the *whole* child.

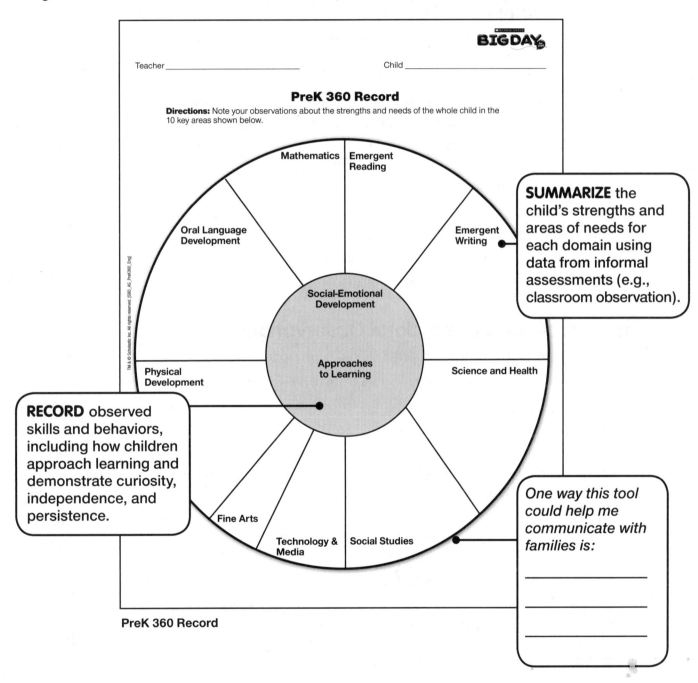

SUMMARIZE the child's strengths and areas of needs for each domain using data from informal assessments (e.g., classroom observation).

RECORD observed skills and behaviors, including how children approach learning and demonstrate curiosity, independence, and persistence.

One way this tool could help me communicate with families is:

Keeping Anecdotal Records

Maintain an ongoing record of children's interactions with other children, with adults, and with their environment to help you track growth over time.

What Are Anecdotal Records?

Anecdotal Records are brief, factual accounts of specific events you observe in a child's day. You can record anything that might provide insight into the child's behavior or development.

In *Big Day for PreK*, you can download and print a blank Anecdotal Record to write down observations or enter and save Anecdotal Records online in Teacher Space (see page 69). Whether entering them online or by hand, be sure to include the following key information each time you record an observation:

- Date of observed event
- Time of day
- Where and when the event took place
- A detailed, objective description of the event
- Reflection on the significance of the event

Best Practices for Anecdotal Observations

Keep these best practices in mind when recording anecdotal observations:

- Note events that reveal something about the child's growth and development.
- Be detailed, accurate, and specific.
- Provide a context for understanding the child's behavior (e.g., when and where it occurred).
- Keep descriptions fact-based and objective (e.g., *Jelani reminded Cris three times that his time was up on the swing.* rather than *Jelani was **impatient** with Cris when he **wouldn't** get off the swing.*).
- Reflect on what the anecdote reveals about the child.

Reflect

Including the date and time in an Anecdotal Record is helpful when updating a child's Pathways to Readiness continuums because:

_____

_____

Recording Anecdotes

Consider the two sample Anecdotal Records below. How do they compare? Use the prompts below to guide your reflection.

Date & Time: 11/29/10, 7:50 am
Context: Blocks & Building Center
Observed Event and Behaviors: When Brett took blocks away from Monique, Cyrus said, "Friends share." Then said, "I bet we can build a big bridge together!" All three children spent the next 10 minutes working together to build a bridge.
Reflection: Cyrus showed a developed sense of social competence. He was able to help peers resolve a conflict and work together.

Sample A

Date & Time: 11/29/10
Context: Learning Centers
Observed Event and Behaviors: Brett snatched a block from Monique. Cyrus stepped in and said something, then convinced everyone to play together.
Reflection: Brett was being rude and Cyrus was able to prevent a fight.

Sample B

1 *The sample Anecdotal Record that reflects best practices is Sample _____ because*

_____

_____.

2 *Two improvements I would make to Sample _____ are _____*

_____

_____

_____

_____.

Big Hint

Jot down anecdotes on sticky notes as they happen, then write a more detailed account later when entering your anecdotes online in Teacher Space.

Creating a Show & Grow Portfolio

Collect children's work and assessment data in Show & Grow Portfolios to document children's growth over time.

What Is Portfolio Assessment?

Portfolios are ongoing, purposeful collections of children's work samples and assessment data. They provide concrete evidence of a child's progress and development over time and across the five Pathways to Readiness domains.

Use the portfolios to help you complete a Clipboard Observation or PreK 360 Record or update the Pathways to Readiness continuums. Share portfolios with families, administrators, or children's future teachers to show what children have accomplished during the school year.

What Do I Include in a Portfolio?

Collect a variety of items throughout the year to give a comprehensive picture of each child's growth and learning during the year.

Individual Observation Tools Include copies of the Pathways to Readiness continuums as well as ongoing Anecdotal Records, Clipboard Observations, and PreK 360 Records.

Formal Assessment Data Include copies of the Scholastic Early Childhood Inventory (SECI) Assessment Records for each administration as well as the child's Progress Report.

Children's Work Samples In prekindergarten, children build, investigate, explore, create, and get hands-on with their environment. In addition to children's artwork and writings, consider including **video clips**, **audio recordings**, and **photographs.**

Big Hint
Get children involved! Have children select their "best" work to include in their portfolios and record their reasons for the selections.

Setting Up Portfolios

Since you will be adding to portfolios throughout the year, be sure to choose organizers that can grow with each child. Some options to consider include:

- Binders with sheet protectors
- File folders or accordion-style folders
- Construction paper bound with twist ties or yarn
- Scrapbooks

Getting Organized

Once you have selected an organizer, the next step is to organize the contents. When organized purposefully, Show & Grow Portfolios can help you plan instruction and communicate progress with families and next year's teachers. Some ideas to consider:

- Organize work samples by developmental areas (e.g., Social-Emotional Development, Oral Language, Emergent Reading, Emergent Writing, Mathematics).
- Include a section for assessment data, such as the SECI Progress Report, Anecdotal Records, Clipboard Observation Guides, and PreK 360 Records.
- Group work by skill and organize in chronological order to easily see growth over time.
- Include a cover note for each item, describing the project or activity, identifying the learning objective, and reflecting on what the sample reveals about the child.

Name: Cris Rodriguez

Date: 11/29/10

Domain/Activity: Math: Making an AB Pattern

Objective: Mimic, Recognize, and Extend AB Patterns

Description: Children were asked to recognize AB auditory, kinesthetic, and visual patterns. Children then created an AB pattern using different colored paper shapes.

Reflection: Cris easily recognized AB patterns and created several sound, motion, and visual patterns of his own. In this example, Cris creates an AB pattern by alternating orange and blue paper.

Sample Cover Note

Portfolios in My Classroom

Use the questions to reflect on how you will use portfolio assessment in your classroom.

1 What materials will you use to create Show & Grow Portfolios? _____

_____

_____

2 What items will you include in Show & Grow Portfolios? _____

_____

_____

3 How will you organize the contents? _____

_____

Monitoring Progress With the Scholastic Early Childhood Inventory

The Scholastic Early Childhood Inventory (SECI) is a formal one-to-one assessment to measure children's developmental progress.

The Scholastic Early Childhood Inventory

The SECI includes four modules, each consisting of two to four subtests that assess specific skills within the key domains.

SECI Module	Subtests	Total Time
Oral Language Development	• Vocabulary • Sentence Structure	10 min./child
Phonological Awareness	• Rhyme Identification • Sound Matching • Phonological Segmentation • Blending	15 min./child
Alphabet Knowledge	• Letter Recognition • Letter Naming Fluency • Letter Sounds	10 min./child
Mathematics	• Number Sense • Geometry • Sorting • Patterns	20 min./child

Administering the SECI

Administer the SECI to 4- or 5-year-olds in a one-to-one setting at **beginning-**, **mid-**, and **end-of-year**. For children who turn 4 during the first half of the school year, administer the SECI only **two** times: first at **mid-year**, then again at the **end-of-year**.

Schedule the SECI over the course of two weeks, administering only one to two modules at a time per child, per day.

Big Hint
Consider administering the Oral Language Development module first. The conversational nature of the module will help "break the ice."

Organizing SECI Materials

Keep all your SECI materials in one place! Download and print the **Teacher Instructions**, **Assessment Records**, and **Child Materials** (in English or Spanish) for each module from Teacher Space (see page 69). Then organize the materials in a special binder for easy reference each time you administer the SECI.

- Print **Teacher Instructions** for each subtest and organize in a three-ring binder.

- Store multiple copies of the teacher **Assessment Records** for each subtest in a labeled three-hole-punched folder or sheet protector within your assessment binder.

- Laminate **Child Materials** for durability and store in a labeled three-hole-punched folder or sheet protector within your assessment binder.

- Use tabs to organize Teacher Instructions, Child Materials, and Assessment Records for each subtest by **module** for easy reference.

- Include a **calendar** in the front of the binder to keep track of scheduled administrations.

Best Practices for Assessing Young Learners

Use the following tips to ensure accurate and meaningful results when administering the SECI. Refer to the Assessment section of your *Professional Handbook* and the Teacher Instructions of each module for more information.

- Download and print the SECI materials (Teacher Instructions, Assessment Records, and Child Materials) from Teacher Space in advance.

- Review SECI materials before each administration.

- Administer the SECI in a comfortable setting with minimal distractions.

- While administering the SECI, stay positive and enthusiastic regardless of the child's responses.

- Pay attention to the child's mood and postpone the assessment if needed.

- Download and print Assessment Records to record each child's score when administering the test, then log in to Teacher Space soon after to enter scores online.

Scoring the SECI

The SECI includes downloadable Assessment Records to help you score each subtest within a module. Read the Teacher Instructions and Assessment Records before administering a test so that you know what information to record. Refer to the Scoring Guidance examples at the end of the Assessment Records for help with scoring.

Once you have completed the Assessment Records for a module, log in to Teacher Space **(http://bigday.scholastic.com)** to enter SECI results online (see page 70).

Big Hint

See *Professional Handbook* pages 84–95 for more information on administering and scoring the SECI and generating SECI reports.

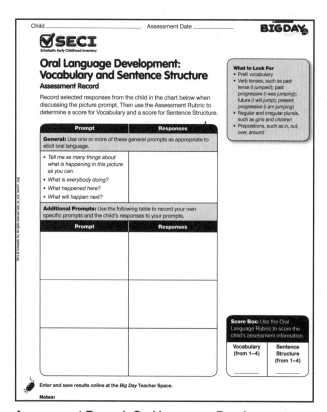

Assessment Record: Oral Language Development

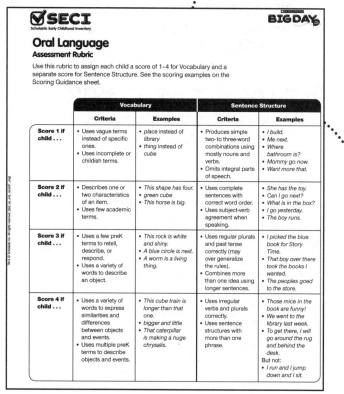

Using SECI Reports

Run and print SECI reports on Teacher Space to help you monitor children's development and communicate progress throughout the year.

Generating SECI Reports

Once you have entered children's assessment scores online, Teacher Space will automatically organize the data into useful reports to help you plan instruction and communicate with administrators and families. Refer to the chart below for guidance when selecting SECI reports.

SECI Report	Description	Purpose
Class Readiness Reports • Oral Language Development • Phonological Awareness • Alphabet Knowledge • Mathematics	Four class-level reports, one for each SECI module, that summarize overall class performance	• Share results with administrators. • Identify children's needs and set learning goals. • Monitor development over time.
Progress Report	Child-level report that shows performance on each subtest for all modules	• Communicate progress with families. • Plan individualized instruction. • Monitor development over time. • Update Pathways to Readiness continuums. • Update Show & Grow Portfolios.
Assessment Status Report	Class-level report that shows which modules each child has completed.	• Schedule SECI administrations • Share information with administrators
Score Record	Child-level report that shows raw scores for each subtest.	• Share information about a child's growth over time. • Gain perspective on Progress Report data. • Plan individualized instruction.

Big Hint

To view all online data for one child, click **View Folder** to the right of a child's name in the **Class Management** screen on Teacher Space.

Class Readiness Reports

Run these reports for a class-level snapshot of children's progress in Oral Language Development, Phonological Awareness, Alphabet Knowledge, and Mathematics.

■ SCHOLASTIC BIG DAY for PreK — **Class Readiness Report: Oral Language Development** — ✓ **SECI** Scholastic Early Childhood Inventory

Teacher: Mr. Martinez
Class: Morning Class
Date: 05/21/10

SUMMARY: Vocabulary	Pre-Emergent	Beginning	Emerging	Developed	Not Tested
Beginning of Year	60%	20%	0%	0%	20%
Middle of Year	20%	20%	40%	10%	10%
End of Year	0%	0%	20%	80%	0%

Individual Performance	Beginning of Year	Middle of Year	End of Year
Anderson, Cyrus	P	B	D
Hutchinson, Adrienne	—	P	E
Johnson, Monique	P	E	D
Lee, Christina	B	D	D
Mensah, Jelani	P	E	E
Moore, Brett	—	B	D
Padilla, Alexandra	P	—	D
Rodriguez, Cris	P	E	D
Tarrell, Dontaira	B	P	D
Valadez, Chad	P	E	D

SUMMARY: Sentence Structure	Pre-Emergent	Beginning	Emerging	Developed	Not Tested
Beginning of Year	70%	10%	0%	0%	20%
Middle of Year	20%	40%	30%	0%	10%
End of Year	0%	10%	70%	20%	0%

Individual Performance	Beginning of Year	Middle of Year	End of Year
Anderson, Cyrus	P	B	E
Hutchinson, Adrienne	—	P	E
Johnson, Monique	P	E	D
Lee, Christina	B	E	D
Mensah, Jelani	P	E	E
Moore, Brett	—	B	E
Padilla, Alexandra	P	—	E
Rodriguez, Cris	P	B	E
Tarrell, Dontaira	P	P	B
Valadez, Chad	P	B	E

Using This Report

Use this report to share information about children's development in oral language.

Legend

P Pre-Emergent B Beginning E Emerging D Developed

Class Readiness Report: Oral Language Development

Taking A Closer Look

Use the following steps to guide your exploration of the Class Readiness Report: Oral Language Development. Then use the report data to complete the information below.

1 Circle the **Legend**. Children's results are reported using the following **four**

developmental stages: _____, _____,

_____, and _____ .

2 Place a star next to the **SUMMARY** box for each sub-test. Then find the following information:

- The percentage of children in the **Pre-Emergent** stage for Vocabulary at the

  beginning of the year: _____

- The percentage of children in the **Developed** stage for Vocabulary at the end of

  the year: _____

- The percentage of children in the **Beginning** stage for Sentence Structure at the

  end of year: _____

3 _____ and _____ were in the **Developed** stage for Sentence Structure by the end of the year.

Using This Report

Use the questions below to reflect on how you might use the report data to identify learning needs and plan next steps.

1 How might you support children who were in the Pre-Emergent stage at the middle of the year?

_____

_____

_____

2 What next steps would you take to support Dontaira at the end of the year?

_____

_____

_____

Progress Report

Generate this report for a skill-by-skill breakdown of a child's progress on each subtest within each SECI module.

SCHOLASTIC BIG DAY for PreK   **Progress Report**    **SECI** Scholastic Early Childhood Inventory

Teacher: Mr. Martinez
Class: Morning Class
Student: Rodriguez, Cris

Date: 05/21/10

	Beginning of Year	Middle of Year	End of Year
Oral Language Development			
Vocabulary	P	E	D
Sentence Structure	P	B	E
Phonological Awareness			
Rhyme Identification	P	D	D
Sound Matching	B	E	D
Segmentation	P	B	E
Blending	P	B	E
Alphabet Knowledge			
Letter Recognition	–	E	D
Letter Naming Fluency	–	D	D
Letter Sounds	–	E	D
Mathematics			
Number Sense	P	B	E
Geometry	P	B	D
Sorting	B	D	D
Patterns	–	B	E

Using This Report
Use this report to share information about this child's growth.

Legend

P Pre-Emergent   B Beginning   E Emerging   D Developed

Progress Report

Taking a Closer Look

Use the following steps to guide your exploration of Cris Rodriguez's Progress Report. Then use Cris's report data to find the information below.

1 Number each **Module**. At the end of the year, Cris's scores placed him in the **Developed** stage for *all* subtests in the following **module**: _____

2 The **two subtests** that Cris performed best on at the **beginning of the year**: _____ and _____.

3 The **three subtests** that Cris performed best in **middle of year**:

_____, _____, and _____.

Using This Report

Use the questions below to reflect on how you might use the report data to communicate with families, plan instruction, and monitor development over time.

1 What would you say about Cris's developmental progress when communicating with his family at the end of the year?

_____

_____

_____

_____

_____

2 What information would you want to share with Cris's kindergarten teacher?

_____

_____

_____

_____

_____

Getting Ready for Kindergarten

The end of the year is a time to reflect on achievements and prepare children for a successful year in kindergarten.

Good-bye, PreK!

Most children have likely bonded with you and their peers and may find it difficult to say good-bye to PreK. After all, you created a safe and warm learning environment where children played, explored, and interacted with friends on a daily basis! To reflect on the year's learning and ease the transition to kindergarten, consider the following ideas:

Create a Class Book Include photographs taken throughout the year. Share the book during whole-group time and use the photographs to prompt children to revisit their learning and reflect on the year.

Create a Keepsake Book Create a personalized book for each child to keep as a memento. Include photos of the child during classroom activities. If you know the child's next teacher, include a photo of him or her as well.

Share Portfolios Allow children an opportunity to share their Show & Grow Portfolios with others. Consider storing portfolios in the Reading & Listening Center, having children present a favorite project during whole-group time, or invite families to an "exhibition" event.

Hello, Kindergarten!

You have collected data and monitored progress all year long. Now that children are about to enter kindergarten, what do you do with all that information?

For Children Use the Show & Grow Portfolios to help children reflect on the year's learning and discuss what they can expect in kindergarten.

For Families Share end-of-year PreK 360 Records and updated Pathways to Readiness continuums with families to discuss children's achievements and suggest ways to continue learning all summer long.

For Teachers Gather key assessment data (e.g., SECI Progress Reports, Anecdotal Records, Clipboard Observation Guides) to pass along to each child's kindergarten teacher. This information will help the child's new teacher gain a better understanding of his or her strengths and learning needs.

Starting a Big Year

Getting Started Time Line

Use the time line to help you prepare your classroom, introduce yourself to children and families, and get ready for a big year with **Big Day for PreK!**

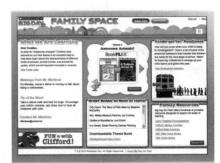

Get Organized! (p. 106)

- Arrange your classroom
- Organize materials
- Create literacy-rich walls

Get Together! (p. 107)

- Lead families on a classroom tour
- Introduce *Big Day for PreK*
- Introduce Family Space and BookFlix

2 Weeks Before PreK

1 Week Before PreK

Get in Touch! (p. 106)

- Send letters to children and families
- Schedule a Family Night

Get Online! (p. 107)

- Set up rosters in Teacher Space
- Post a welcome message on Family Space
- Download and print the Theme 1 Family Letter

Get Ready for the First Big Day! (p. 107)

- Review lessons in *Theme 1 Teaching Guide*
- Gather teaching materials and resources
- Set up theme-specific Learning Center activities
- Plan ways to engage families and community

Get Acquainted! (p. 108)
- Get to know each other
- Tour the classroom with children
- Introduce the daily schedule

Get Information! (p. 108)
- Begin administering SECI
- Use informal assessment tools
- Place children along Pathways to Readiness

PreK Week 1

PreK Week 2

Get Started With Theme 1! (p. 108)
- Introduce routines and expectations
- Introduce Learning Centers
- Introduce vocabulary

Get Started With BookFlix! (p. 108)
- Introduce Technology Center
- Introduce BookFlix

Beginning-of-Year Checklists

*Use these checklists to help you prepare as you countdown to the first **big** day and begin the school year!*

Two Weeks Before the Big Day

Organize your classroom and introduce yourself to children and their families.

Get Organized

❑ Arrange your classroom for **whole-group Circle Time and Story Time, Small Group Instruction**, and **Learning Centers** (pages 48–49).

❑ Make sure your classroom is a **safe**, child-friendly environment (pages 46–47).

❑ Separate Learning Centers with child-friendly **furniture** and low **bookshelves** (pages 43–45).

❑ **Label** key areas of the room (e.g., Technology Center) and names of objects (e.g., table, shelf) to build children's vocabulary.

❑ **Organize materials** in easily accessible, clearly labeled storage bins (pages 43–45).

❑ Provide space (e.g., individual cubbies) for children to **store their belongings**.

❑ Display **posters** (e.g., Big Wall Chart, Be Big in the Classroom poster, Alphabet Frieze) in central areas of the room.

❑ Post the **daily schedule** in the Circle Time/Story Time area (page 51).

❑ Prepare **bulletin boards** to showcase children's work.

Get in Touch

❑ Print and make copies of the **Family Welcome Letter** (in English or Spanish) from Teacher Space (page 67). Mail it to the families of your incoming class.

❑ Write an **introductory letter or postcard** to send to each child (page 113).

❑ Print and complete a **Family Invitation** template (in English or Spanish) from Teacher Space (page 67) to invite children and their families to an Open House before the first day of school.

Big Hint
Keep classroom walls relatively bare at the start of the year. Soon you will need the space to showcase children's masterpieces!

Family Welcome Letter

One Week Before the Big Day

Before school starts, invite children and families into your classroom to build enthusiasm for the **big** year ahead! Then use Teacher Space to plan and prepare for a successful start!

Get Together

- ❑ Review the **Home to School** and **School to Home** suggestions in the Engaging Families and the Community pages of your *Theme 1 Teaching Guide* so you can get families engaged from day 1 (page 21).

- ❑ Print and make copies of the **About Family Space Family Letter** (in English or Spanish) from Teacher Space (page 67). Remember to write down the **Class Username and Password** so families can log in to Family Space!

- ❑ Print and make copies of the **Reinforcing Vocabulary at Home Family Letter** (in English or Spanish) from Teacher Space and distribute during Open House (page 67).

- ❑ Give families a **tour of the classroom**, introduce them to *Big Day for PreK*, and explain what the **child's day** will look like.

- ❑ Make children feel welcome by placing a **special note** in each cubby for children to discover during the classroom tour.

- ❑ Distribute the About Family Space Letter and project **Family Space** and **BookFlix** onto a screen or interactive whiteboard to highlight key features (pages 114–116).

Get Online

- ❑ Log in to Teacher Space to **create your classes** and **add students** to your rosters (page 65).

- ❑ Display the **Theme 1 Letter** and **Tip of the Week** on Family Space (page 71).

- ❑ Post a **welcome message** for families to read on Family Space (page 71).

Get Ready for the First Big Day

- ❑ Review **Theme 1 lessons** in your *Theme 1 Teaching Guide*.

- ❑ Review the **Learning Centers tab** of your *Theme 1 Teaching Guide* for ideas to set up theme-specific activities in each Center (pages 22–23).

- ❑ Schedule **Field Trips** and **Classroom Visitors** using the suggestions in the Engaging Families and the Community pages in your *Theme 1 Teaching Guide* (page 21).

- ❑ Plan a class trip to the **school or community library.**

PreK Week 1

Hooray! The first big day has arrived! Use the ideas below for a successful start of the year!

Get Acquainted

❏ Use the Week 1 lessons in your *Theme 1 Teaching Guide* to **introduce yourself** and **introduce children** to each other.

❏ Introduce the **daily class schedule** and model how to use the interactive display (pages 50–52).

❏ Provide children with a guided **tour of the school**, visiting key places such as the principal's office, nurse's office, playground, and bathrooms.

❏ Invite **school personnel** (e.g., principal, crossing guard, nurse) to your classroom to introduce themselves and explain their role at the school.

Get Started With Theme 1

❏ Use the *Theme 1 Teaching Guide* lessons to set **expectations** and gradually introduce **daily routines** and **Learning Centers** (pages 122–126).

❏ Refer to the **Vocabulary** page at the end of the weekly lesson plan in your *Theme 1 Teaching Guide* to help you reinforce theme vocabulary throughout the day.

❏ Create a **Word Wall** using the Theme 1 **Vocabulary Cutouts,** downloadable from Teacher Space (page 67). Send a copy home with families, too!

❏ Use the **Theme Conversations** suggestions at the start of your *Theme 1 Teaching Guide* to engage children with the theme topic at any time.

PreK Week 2

Spend time in your second week learning more about your children!

Get Information

❏ Use a **three-ring binder with tabs** to organize SECI materials (e.g., Teacher Instructions, Assessment Records, Child Materials) for easy reference (page 95).

❏ Schedule one-to-one administration of **SECI** to establish **baseline scores** (page 94).

❏ Print **Classroom Observation Guides** from Teacher Space to informally assess children in whole- and small-group settings during the week (pages 68, 84–87).

❏ Enter daily **Anecdotal Records** online using Teacher Space (pages 69, 90–91).

❏ Use initial assessment data and family input to place children along **Pathways to Readiness** continuums (pages 82–83).

❏ Create **Show & Grow Portfolios** to gather children's work samples as they learn and grow all year long (pages 92–93).

Get Started With BookFlix

❏ Bookmark BookFlix on the Web browser for each **Technology Center computer** and save the Class Username and Class Password for easy login (page 64).

❏ Project BookFlix on a screen or interactive whiteboard during whole-group time to **model how to navigate** the site (pages 74–76, 116).

Making a First Impression

Build relationships with children and families early on. Make a positive impression by introducing yourself before the school year begins.

Sending Letters Home

Help build enthusiasm for the year ahead by reaching out to children and families *before* the school year starts!

In addition to sending home the Family Welcome Letter (downloadable from Teacher Space) to introduce families to the **big** year ahead, you might also:

- Write a personal note to introduce yourself (and your colleagues) and set expectations.
- Request photographs of each child to create a class display and personalize each child's cubby space.
- Send a separate note or postcard to each child to welcome him or her to PreK.

Making Phone Calls

Consider calling children and their families to get acquainted, answer questions, and possibly schedule a home or classroom visit. Complete the sample script below to help you get started!

Hello, this is _____. I will be _____'s preschool teacher this year and am looking forward to having him/her in my class! I am calling to share a little about myself and the big year ahead! Do you have a moment to talk?

To tell you a little about myself, I ...

_____

_____

This year, I'll be teaching *Big Day for PreK!* In *Big Day for PreK,* children will ...

_____

_____

Is there anything you would like me to know about your son/daughter? Do you have any questions or concerns to share?

Sample Script, English

Hola, soy _____. Yo seré la maestra preescolar de _____ este año y ¡me hace ilusión tenerle en mi clase! ¡Estoy llamando para compartir un poco sobre mí y el gran año que viene! ¿Tiene usted un momento para hablar?

Para contar un poco sobre mí, yo ...

_____

_____

¡Este año, estaré enseñando Big Day for PreK! En Big Day for PreK, los niños ...

_____

_____

¿Hay algo que me serviría bien saber de su niño/a? ¿Tiene usted alguna pregunta o preocupación que compartir?

Sample Script, Spanish

Scheduling Home Visits

Home visits can be reassuring for both children and their families and provide an opportunity for you to learn more about the children in your class. If you plan to visit children's homes, call families to schedule a visit as soon as you receive your class lists. Plan to spend about 30 minutes per visit bonding with each child.

Consider the suggestions below as you prepare. Then add some ideas of your own.

- Bring a photo album of your classroom. Use the photographs to help families and children know what they can expect each day. Point out where children will sign in, store their belongings, and gather for Morning Meeting. If possible, include photos of projects and activities from previous years to get children excited about school!

- Bring Clifford along! Explain that Clifford is about to start school, too. Allow children to talk with the Clifford puppet about their upcoming first day of school. Reassure children that their new friend will be in the classroom each day, too!

- Conduct a brief interest survey. Ask children to share three favorites, such as their favorite color, book, and food. Record their responses and take a picture of each child. Attach the child's picture to their list of favorites to display in the classroom.

- Take along a favorite book to share and read aloud with children, such as *Owen, My New School,* or *Clifford's First School Day*. Explain that they will get to read and listen to stories every day at school!

- _____

  _____

- _____

  _____

Big Hint

Administrators may have different policies on home visits. If you are unsure of the policy at your school, speak with your administrator for clarification.

Welcoming Children and Families

Ease the transition from home to school by inviting children and their families to visit your classroom before the first day of PreK.

A Great Start

Starting preschool can be an emotional experience for children and the caring adults in their lives. For young children, going to school can be both exciting and stressful. Children might wonder, *What will school be like? Who will I play with? Will I like my teacher?* For families, sending children to their first day of school can be just as emotional. Families might wonder, *Is this classroom safe for my child? What will my child learn this year? How will I know how my child is doing?*

In addition to sending a friendly welcome letter or making an introductory phone call, consider inviting families into your classroom *before* the first **big** day!

Inviting Families Into Your Classroom

Before the first day of school, invite children and their families to an Open House to get them excited about the year ahead and feel more at ease!

To get started, download, print, and complete the Family Invitation template (in English or Spanish) from Teacher Space (see page 67). Mail the invitations at least two weeks before school starts.

Big Hint
Continue to use the Family Invitation template throughout the year to invite families to **Family Workshops** or **Parent-Teacher Conferences.**

Family Invitation, English

Family Invitation, Spanish

Hosting an Open House

Provide children and families a sneak peek into the year ahead by hosting an Open House. Use the Open House to introduce yourself, tour the classroom, review your daily schedule, answer questions, and share your excitement for the upcoming year with *Big Day for PreK*.

Once you have sent the invitations, the next step is to prepare! Consider the following activities to connect with families during Open House:

Activity	Description	Purpose	Materials Needed
Family Portrait	Take a picture of each child with his or her family. Display one copy of the photo on a family bulletin board and send another copy home for families to keep.	• Provides a visual reminder of the home-school partnership • Comforts children who may miss family during the school day	• Digital camera
Introduce *Big Day for PreK*	Get your classroom school-ready so children and families can see the learning environment. Gather *Big Day for PreK* materials that children will use throughout the year.	• Helps children and families know what to expect • Gets children and families excited about the year!	• *Theme 1 Teaching Guide* • *Songs & Fingerplays* CD • Clifford books and puppet • Manipulatives (e.g., snap cubes, magnetic healthy food kit) • Read aloud books
Introduce Family Space and BookFlix	Show families and children how to access the technology. Highlight key features and practice navigating the websites.	• Gives families and children the information necessary to get started using online resources • Makes families feel comfortable using the technology	• Computer with Internet connection • Projector • Screen or interactive whiteboard • About Family Space Family Letter (download from Teacher Space)

Reflect: Welcoming Children and Families

Consider the ways you can make everyone feel welcome and at home in your classroom. Use the acrostic below to reflect on how you might help ease the transition to school for children and their families.

W <u>rite introductory letters to children and families.</u>

E _____

L _____

C _____

O _____

M _____

E _____

Introducing Family Space

Support families early on with a guided tour of Family Space—the incredible online resource and bilingual communication tool to help families stay connected all year!

About Family Space

Family Space is a bilingual communication tool that offers families a virtual window into their child's learning and includes resources for families to extend learning at home. Parents and caregivers can log in to Family Space (**http://bigdayfamily.scholastic.com**) from any computer with an Internet connection using the Class Username and Class Password you created (see page 64). From the Home Page, families can:

- Learn what is going on in the classroom.
- Access a variety of downloadable books and resources (in English and Spanish).
- Download Kindergarten Readiness Indicators to track children's developmental milestones at home.

So how do you get the word out about this great online resource? Download the **About Family Space Letter** (in English or Spanish) from Teacher Space. Write down the Class Username and Class Password you created when setting up your classes in Teacher Space so families can access Family Space and BookFlix.

Big Hint

Forgot the class login? Look it up on **Teacher Space**! Click **View Class Data** under **Class Management,** then look for the Class Username and Password on the left.

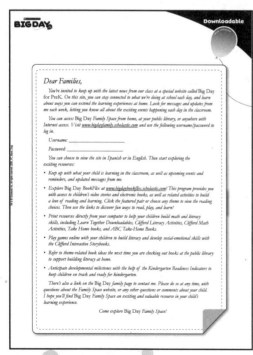

About Family Space Letter, English

About Family Space Letter, Spanish

Navigating Family Space

During Open House, distribute the About Family Space Letter. Then project Family Space (**http://bigdayfamily.scholastic.com**) onto a screen or interactive whiteboard. Spend a few minutes on the Home Page, pointing out key areas. If projecting the website onto an interactive whiteboard, invite volunteers to use the board to navigate the site.

Use the space provided below to note what key features of Family Space you plan to highlight at Open House.

Big Hint

Refer to *Professional Handbook* pages 36–39 for more information on the tools and resources available on Family Space.

Two things I would point out in **What We Are Learning** *are:*

_____

_____

One reason I suggest families download the **Kindergarten Readiness Indicators** *is:*

_____

_____

FAMILY SPACE

SCHOLASTIC BIG DAY   ENGLISH   ESPANOL   Sign out | Help

What We Are Learning

Dear Families,
It's time for "Awesome Animals!" Children love animals so our new theme is an excellent way to help them learn about the characteristics of different kinds of animals, animal homes, and animal life cycles, which are all important concepts in science.

View Family Letter

Message from Mr. Martinez
On Monday, Aaron's father is coming to talk about being a veterinarian.

Tip of the Week
Take a nature walk and look for bugs. Encourage your child's curiosity, and show how to treat all creatures with care.

Contact Mr. Martinez
JMartinez@school.net

FUN with Clifford!

Theme 4
Awesome Animals!
BookFLIX
Watch the Story! Read the Book!
THE CALENDAR   *A Tadpole Grows Up*
GO
Browse All

Great Books to Read at Home!

City Hawk: The Story of Pale Male by Meghan McCarthy
Mrs. Wishy-Washy's Farm by Joy Cowley
Oodles of Noodles by Lois Ehlert
In a Small, Small Pond by Denise Fleming

Downloadable Theme Book
Old MacDonald Had a Farm

Kindergarten Readiness

How will you know when your child is ready for Kindergarten? Here's a list of some of the preschool behaviors that indicate that children are ready for the next stage of school. Watch for these key milestones to emerge as your child learns and grows this year.

View Kindergarten Indicators

Family Resources

Big Day for PreK offers hundreds of printable resources designed to support all areas of learning.

Learn Together Downloadables
Clifford Literacy Activities
Clifford Math Activities
ABC Take Home Books
Take Home Books

Browse All

Family Space Home Page

One thing I will say about reading books at home is:

_____

_____

Two resources I will preview are:

_____

_____

Exploring BookFlix

Get children and families excited about BookFlix, the online literacy resource with video storybooks and nonfiction eBooks related to each *Big Day for PreK* theme. Click GO in the BookFlix icon at the center of the Family Space Home Page to go to BookFlix. Spend a few minutes giving children and families a tour using a projected image. As you explore the site together, point out some of the following features:

- Children and families can view the site in English or Spanish.

- Clicking the **Family** link at the top of the BookFlix Home Page will direct families to an overview of BookFlix, with guidance for using the online resources with children.

- For each theme, BookFlix includes two fiction/nonfiction Reading Pairs. That's 16 Reading Pairs in total.

- Reading Pairs consist of one video storybook and one nonfiction eBook with a read aloud feature.

- When reading an eBook, children can place their mouse cursor over key content vocabulary words highlighted in yellow to view a definition. They can click the ear icon to hear the definition read aloud.

BookFlix Home Page

- Each Reading Pair includes **Puzzlers!**, or interactive educational games related to the video storybook and/or eBook.

- Families can browse all titles by clicking **Browse All** in the bottom right corner of the Home Page.

Explain that you might use BookFlix in the classroom during Story Time or that children can use BookFlix independently in the Technology Center during Learning Centers. Outside of school, families can access BookFlix from any computer with Internet access (e.g., at home, in a library) to engage children in literacy fun!

Big Hint

Consider hosting Family Workshops during the year to revisit BookFlix and guide families to read aloud, talk about stories, and make the most of online resources.

Developing a Home-School Connection

Build a partnership with families early on to support children's learning year-round.

The Importance of Family

Children enter preschool with the experiences and knowledge they learned from their families. As prekindergartners, children will spend a significant amount of time with their school "family." Both families will play a significant role in a young learner's growth and development. So it is important that teachers and families come together to help children build a strong foundation in literacy and learning at school and at home.

Engaging families throughout the year is a key component of *Big Day for PreK*. Research shows that maintaining positive home-to-school connections has a lasting impact on children's learning and development. Consider the research below, then use the prompts in the second column to guide your reflection.

Research	Reflection
Young children experience greater school readiness and later academic success when their families are meaningfully engaged in their early learning (Halgunseth et al., 2009).	*Two ways* Big Day for PreK *helps me engage families throughout the year are . . .* _____ _____ *and* _____ _____ .
Shared reading of books in the home during preschool years has been linked with emergent literacy skills, language development, and later reading success (Arnold et al., 2008).	*Two ways I can support families reading to their children at home include . . .* _____ _____ *and* _____ _____ .
Home-school connections can help families better understand their children's particular strengths as learners and specific methods to support their learning at home (Frede, 1998).	*One way I can help families track and support their child's learning is . . .* _____ _____ .

Engaging Families All Year Long

Once you have established a home-school connection, it is important to maintain that connection throughout the year.

Communicate Online Update your message on Family Space on a weekly basis. Let families know about classroom activities (e.g., *On Tuesday, we will learn all about the letter Hh.*), events (e.g., *On Thursday, Helena, our school crossing guard, will explain how to safely cross the street.*), or reminders (e.g., *Remember this is the last week before break!*).

Keep Them Posted! Create a family bulletin board near the entry. Post a class calendar highlighting key events for families to see when dropping off and picking up their children. Consider also including announcements or flyers about family events in the community.

Invite Families to the Classroom Refer to the Engaging Families and Community pages at the start of each theme *Teaching Guide* for suggestions to involve families in theme learning. Family members can also help out in other ways, such as by chaperoning a field trip, organizing a celebration, or helping prepare a snack.

Schedule Family Conferences Meet with parents and guardians to share your observations of their child's development, using the SECI Progress Report, Anecdotal Records, or the PreK 360 Record to help guide the conversation. Then have families share their own observations for a comprehensive understanding of the child's progress as a whole.

Reflect

One way I plan to engage families at the start of the year is:

_____

_____

One idea I have to stay connected with families throughout the year is:

_____

_____

The First Day of School

Now the first day of school has arrived! Consider how you will get the school year off to a good start.

Transitioning From Home to School

The first day of school can be overwhelming for both children and families. The time devoted to reaching out to children and families before the year begins helps to ease the transition. Even so, some children may feel anxious when the time comes for their parents or caregivers to depart. Consider the scenarios below and reflect on how you might support these children as they transition to school.

Scenario A

Cris hides behind his grandma as he nears the classroom entrance. His grandma notices the **welcome** poster outside the classroom and points out Cris's name and photo. Cris points to the picture of himself, but continues to grip his grandma's hand tightly.

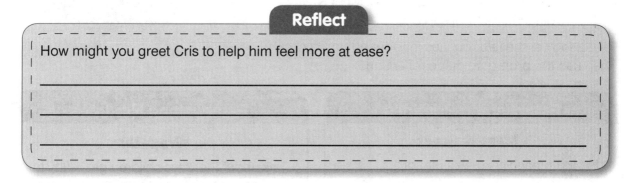

Reflect

How might you greet Cris to help him feel more at ease?

_____

_____

_____

Scenario B

Monique walks into the classroom and leads her dad to the Creativity Center. She draws quietly as her dad sits with her. When he gets up to leave, tears well in Monique's eyes and she runs after him.

Reflect

What would you say to Monique?

_____

_____

_____

Introducing Routines

Establishing routines and expectations is key to a successful year. Routines help children feel secure in knowing what to expect during the day. *Big Day for PreK* includes:

Meet & Greet Routines Use these routines in the morning to welcome children, take attendance, or discuss the day.

Engagement Routines Help children get involved! Use these routines to get children actively participating in the classroom.

Wrap Up Routines Help children wind down, reflect, and transition from school-to-home with these end-of-day routines.

The *Theme 1 Teaching Guide* lessons help you gradually introduce just a few routines at a time, one step at a time, with opportunities to practice and review throughout the week. On the first day of school, the *Theme 1 Teaching Guide* guides you to introduce part of the Arrive at School Meet & Greet Routine and the Going Home Wrap-Up Routine.

Take a look at the two routines introduced on Day 1. Then use the prompt to guide reflection.

Big Hint
See *Professional Handbook* pages 24–29 for step-by-step guidance for using the Meet & Greet, Wrap-Up, and Engagement Routines.

Establishing Routines
Meet & Greet

Explicitly teach children a part of the morning routine by prompting a volunteer to greet you with a wave. Then show children the cubbies where they should place their backpacks in the morning. Point out each child's name on his or her cubby.

USES CLASSROOM RULES AND ROUTINES

Theme 1 Teaching Guide, Week 1, Monday

Establishing Routines
Wrap-Up

Talk about the ways children get ready to go home. Model how to put things away, say goodbye to the teacher and friends, get things from the cubby, and line up at the door. Be sure children know if they need to be in a special place when their caretakers arrive and how to respond when they come.

USES CLASSROOM RULES AND ROUTINES

Theme 1 Teaching Guide, Week 1, Monday

Reflect

One benefit of introducing routines gradually is:

_____

_____

Starting Theme 1

Start using your Theme 1 Teaching Guide *from the very first day of school.*

An Introduction

The *Theme 1 Teaching Guide* is different from the other themes in its focus on slowly establishing routines and expectations. It is an introduction not only to the theme topic, My School, but also includes built-in support for introducing children to daily routines and activities in the daily schedule.

Take a look at the Day at a Glance for the first day of the school year: Theme 1, Week 1, Monday. How does this day compare to the Day at a Glance page from the *Theme 3 Teaching Guide* on page 20? Circle any differences you notice.

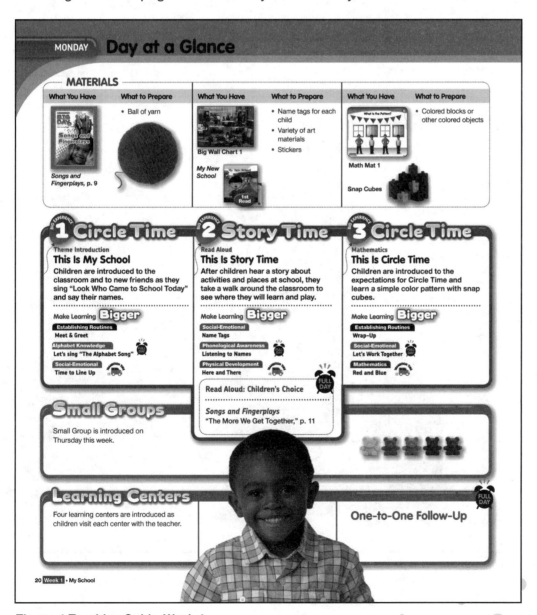

Theme 1 Teaching Guide, Week 1

Starting a Big Year

Your First Week

Review the Week 1 Overview pages from the Theme 1 Teaching Guide *as you prepare to gradually introduce children to the daily activities and routines.*

The **Week 1 Knowledge Focus** is important because:

_____

_____

_____

The routines I will introduce during Week 1 are:

_____

_____

_____

_____

_____

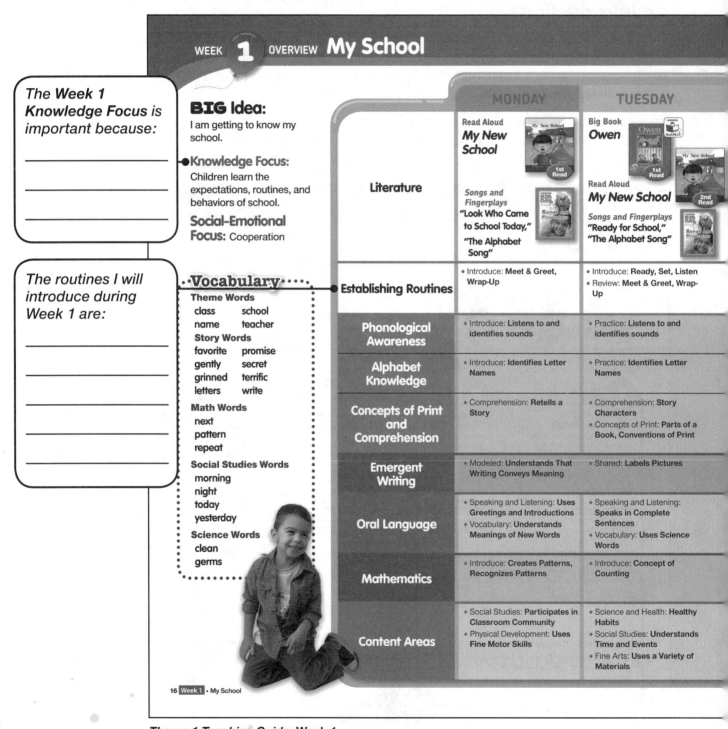

WEEK 1 OVERVIEW My School

BIG Idea:
I am getting to know my school.

Knowledge Focus:
Children learn the expectations, routines, and behaviors of school.

Social-Emotional Focus: Cooperation

Vocabulary

Theme Words
class   school
name   teacher

Story Words
favorite   promise
gently   secret
grinned   terrific
letters   write

Math Words
next
pattern
repeat

Social Studies Words
morning
night
today
yesterday

Science Words
clean
germs

16 Week 1 • My School

	MONDAY	TUESDAY
Literature	Read Aloud *My New School* (1st Read) Songs and Fingerplays "Look Who Came to School Today," "The Alphabet Song"	Big Book *Owen* (1st Read) Read Aloud *My New School* (2nd Read) Songs and Fingerplays "Ready for School," "The Alphabet Song"
Establishing Routines	• Introduce: **Meet & Greet, Wrap-Up**	• Introduce: **Ready, Set, Listen** • Review: **Meet & Greet, Wrap-Up**
Phonological Awareness	• Introduce: **Listens to and identifies sounds**	• Practice: **Listens to and identifies sounds**
Alphabet Knowledge	• Introduce: **Identifies Letter Names**	• Practice: **Identifies Letter Names**
Concepts of Print and Comprehension	• Comprehension: **Retells a Story**	• Comprehension: **Story Characters** • Concepts of Print: **Parts of a Book, Conventions of Print**
Emergent Writing	• Modeled: **Understands That Writing Conveys Meaning**	• Shared: **Labels Pictures**
Oral Language	• Speaking and Listening: **Uses Greetings and Introductions** • Vocabulary: **Understands Meanings of New Words**	• Speaking and Listening: **Speaks in Complete Sentences** • Vocabulary: **Uses Science Words**
Mathematics	• Introduce: **Creates Patterns, Recognizes Patterns**	• Introduce: **Concept of Counting**
Content Areas	• Social Studies: **Participates in Classroom Community** • Physical Development: **Uses Fine Motor Skills**	• Science and Health: **Healthy Habits** • Social Studies: **Understands Time and Events** • Fine Arts: **Uses a Variety of Materials**

Theme 1 Teaching Guide, Week 1

WEDNESDAY	THURSDAY	FRIDAY
Read Aloud *Owen* 2nd Read **Read Aloud** *The Kissing Hand* 1st Read	**Read Aloud** *The Kissing Hand* 2nd Read · 3rd Read *Songs and Fingerplays* "The Alphabet Song"	**ABC Book** *Annie, Bea, and Chi Chi Dolores* 1st Read *Songs and Fingerplays* "The Alphabet Song"
• Introduce: **Keep Trying** • Review: **Meet & Greet, Ready, Set, Listen, Wrap-Up**	• Introduce: **Think, Turn, and Talk** • Review: **Meet & Greet, Keep Trying, Wrap-Up**	• Review: **Meet & Greet, Think, Turn, and Talk, Wrap-Up**
• Practice: **Listens to and identifies sounds**	• Practice: **Listens to and identifies sounds**	• Small Groups Practice: **Listens to and identifies sounds**
• Practice: **Identifies Letter Names**	• Small Groups Practice: **Identifies Letter Names**	• Practice: **Identifies Letter Names, Identifies Letter Sounds, Identifies Letters**
• Comprehension: **Story Characters, Retells a Story** • Concepts of Print: **Book Handling**	• Comprehension: **Story Sequence, Uses Book Information, Retells a Story** • Concepts of Print: **Meaning of Print**	• Comprehension: **Makes Predictions**
• Shared: **Contributes Ideas for Writing**	• Modeled: **Uses Writing Conventions** • Independent: **Forms Letters**	• Independent: **Writes Name**
• Speaking and Listening: **Follows Oral Directions** • Vocabulary: **Uses Story Words**	• Speaking and Listening: **Uses Language for Different Purposes** • Vocabulary: **Understands Instructional Language**	• Speaking and Listening: **Engages in Conversation** • Vocabulary: **Uses School Words**
• Practice: **Recognizes Patterns, Creates Patterns**	• Practice: **Recognizes Patterns, Creates Patterns**	• Practice/Draw/Assess: **Recognizes Patterns, Creates Patterns**
• Fine Arts: **Engages in Dramatic Play**	• Science and Health: **Explores Living Things** • Fine Arts: **Uses a Variety of Materials** • Physical Development: **Uses Gross Motor Skills**	• Social Studies: **Participates in Classroom Community** • Fine Arts: **Sings New and Familiar Songs** • Physical Development: **Uses Fine Motor Skills**

BIG DAY Online

For Families

Remind families to share in their child's learning by exploring the *Big Day* Online Family Space for:

- *Big Day* BookFlix videos, multimedia books, and activities
- Tip of the Week
- Theme Letter
- Online Fun and Games
- Learn and Play Downloadables
- Family Resources and more!

AND Access the **Teacher Space** to customize lesson plans, get resources, set up family tips, and more.

Learning Centers

Blocks & Building Center
- Build a school and a home with blocks and use toy vehicles to drive back and forth.

Dramatic Play Center
- Use props and pretend to be the people who work at school, such as the teacher, librarian, crossing guard, or bus driver.

Math Center
- Make colorful AB patterns with crayons.

Reading and Listening Center
- Learn to operate the audio player, and listen to and read along with *Owen* and *My Friends*.

Four more Learning Centers are introduced in Week 2.

> *Why do you think these four Learning Centers are introduced first?*
>
> _____
> _____
> _____

Planning Your First Week

Review the lessons in your *Theme 1 Teaching Guide*, then use the chart to help you plan and navigate the first week.

Class _____   ❑ **Full-Day**   ❑ **AM**   ❑ **PM**

	Activity (TG page)	Materials	Observe
Monday			
Tuesday			
Wednesday			
Thursday			
Friday			

Notes: _____

_____

Scheduling the SECI

Schedule SECI administrations during the first weeks of school to establish a baseline for comparing progress throughout the year. Administer the SECI in a fun, game-like manner module by module, beginning with Oral Language Development. Use the chart below to help you schedule each module.

	SECI Module			
Child's Name	Oral Language Development (10 min.)	Phonological Awareness (15 min.)	Alphabet Knowledge (10 min.)	Mathematics (20 min.)
	Date/Time	Date/Time	Date/Time	Date/Time

On the Path to Readiness

In order to know how to guide children to kindergarten readiness, it is important to first understand where they are along the path. Use the SECI results, your own teacher observations, and family observations to help you place children along the Pathways to Readiness. Refer to pages 82–83 of this book and pages 72–83 in the *Professional Handbook* for more on the Pathways to Readiness continuums.

Download continuums for each child from Teacher Space (see page 67) and store them in children's Show & Grow Portfolios. Use the continuums to guide your selection of children's work samples to include in portfolios.

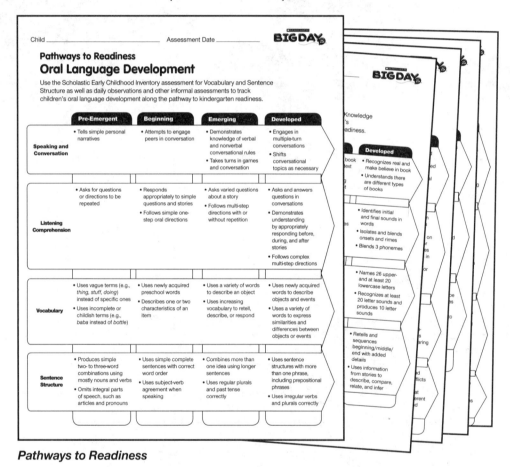

Pathways to Readiness

Reflect

Consider the Pathways to Readiness continuum for Oral Language Development. How will you use the SECI to place a child along the continuum?

_____

_____

What other data could you draw from?

_____

Big Day for PreK
Implementation Training

Evaluation

Name (optional) _____   Date _____

School/District _____   Trainer _____

Please answer the following questions by circling the number, with 1 as lowest and 5 as highest.

	Lowest		Highest		
1. Overall, how satisfied were you with this training?	1	2	3	4	5
2. To what extent did the content meet the stated learning outcomes?	1	2	3	4	5
3. How satisfied were you with (rate all that apply to your training):	1	2	3	4	5
a. Introducing *Big Day for PreK*	1	2	3	4	5
b. Making Learning Bigger!	1	2	3	4	5
c. Managing Your Day	1	2	3	4	5
d. Building Literacy From School to Home	1	2	3	4	5
e. Exploring Teacher Space Online	1	2	3	4	5
f. Watching Children Learn and Grow	1	2	3	4	5
g. Starting a Big Year!	1	2	3	4	5

What recommendations do you have for future *Big Day for PreK* trainings?

_____

_____

_____

What questions do you still have?

_____

_____

_____

Bibliography

Albert Shanker Institute. (2009). *Preschool curriculum*: *What's in it for children and teachers?* Washington, DC: Author.

Halgunseth, L. C., Peterson, A., Stark, D. R., & Moodie, S. (2009). *Family engagement, diverse families, and early childhood education programs: An integrated review of the literature.* Washington, DC: National Association for the Education of Young Children.

Miller, E., & Almon, J. (2009). *Crisis in the kindergarten: Why children need to play in school.* College Park, MD: Alliance for Childhood.

National Research Council. (2001). *Eager to learn: Educating our preschoolers. Committee on Early Childhood Pedagogy.* Washington, DC: The National Academies Press.

National Research Council. (2008). *Early childhood assessment: Why, what, and how. Committee on Developmental Outcomes and Assessments for Young Children.* Washington, DC: The National Academies Press.

National Scientific Council on the Developing Child. (2008). *Science briefs: Focus and planning skills can be improved before a child enters school.* [Online] http://developingchild.harvard.edu/index.php/download_file/-/view/90/

Reynolds, A. J., Temple, J. A., Robertson, D. L., & Mann, E. A. (2001). Long-term effects of an early childhood intervention on educational achievement and juvenile arrest: A 15-year follow-up of low-income children in public schools. *Journal of American Medical Association, 285,* 2339–2346.

Rhode Island KIDS COUNT. (2005). *Getting ready: Findings from the National School Readiness Indicators Initiative.* Providence, RI: Author.

Sandall, S., McLean, M. E., & Smith, B. J. (2000). *DEC recommended practices in early intervention/early childhood special education.* Denver, CO: Division for Early Childhood of the Council for Exceptional Children.

Snow, C. E., Tabors, P. O., Nicholson, P. A., & Kurland, B. F. (1995). SHELL: Oral language and early literacy skills in kindergarten and first-grade children. *Journal of Research in Childhood Education, 10*(1), 37–48.

Strickland, D., & Riley-Ayers, S. (2006). *Early literacy: Policy and practice in the preschool years. National Institute for Early Education Research (NIEER) Preschool Policy Brief.* [Online] http://www.colorincolorado.org/article/11375